A Victorian Floral ALPHABET

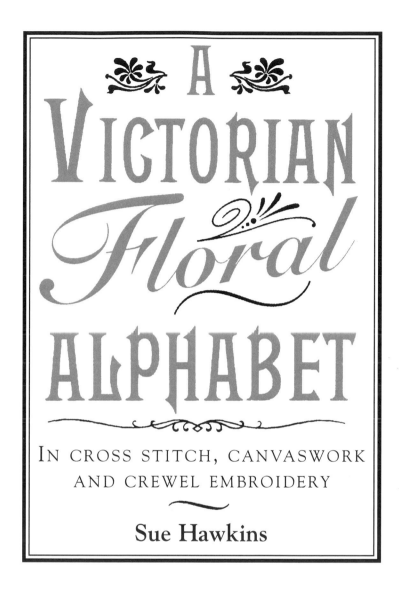

A Victorian Floral ALPHABET

In cross stitch, canvaswork
and crewel embroidery

Sue Hawkins

David & Charles

To the memory of my mother, Pamela,
who taught me to sew before she died
on the 13th June 1960.

Orange blossom pincushion (see page 60).
Page 1: Anemone lavender bag (see page 13).
Page 2: (From top left) viola, nasturtium, anemone,
orange blossom and rose crewel miniatures (see pages
88, 53, 14, 58 and 74).

For Hannah and Jo

A DAVID & CHARLES BOOK

First published in the UK in 1997

Text and designs Copyright © Sue Hawkins 1997
Photography and layout Copyright © David & Charles 1997

Sue Hawkins has asserted her right to be identified as author
of this work in accordance with the Copyright, Designs and
Patents Act, 1988.

A catalogue record for this book is available from
the British Library.

ISBN 0 7153 0466 6

Photography by Tim Hill
Styling by Zöe Hill
Book design by Maggie Aldred
Typeset by ABM Typographics Ltd, Hull
and printed in USA

Contents

Introduction

The Victorian era has always held a fascination for me: the rich, warm colours and sumptuous fabrics; the profusion of hand-crafted items; the way that craftwork was part of everyday life. That fascination was a major inspiration for this book.

Plants were very important to the Victorians. Intrepid travellers were still discovering exotic varieties in all corners of the world; natural remedies were still being used as well as patent medicines. Flowers were a potent design source for most embroiderers, and appeared in different shapes, shades and materials throughout the home. And there developed an intricate, complex language of flowers. To everything there was a meaning; a simple posy could say so much. It's not surprising that, when I wanted to create a book with a Victorian feel, I chose flowers as my theme.

By arranging my projects in this book as an alphabet – one flower for each letter – I am following a typical Victorian style of presentation. It wasn't without its problems, of course. Not all letters are very useful, and I had to 'cheat' a little. (I leave it to you to find out where. Thank goodness, though, for Latin names!)

I have also taken a Victorian approach to making up and mounting completed projects. As you look through the pages of this book I hope you will be struck by how much a piece of embroidery can be enhanced by the way it is mounted or made up. I have always maintained that once the embroidery is finished the job is only half done! The choice of fabric and the trimming of a cushion or the framing of a picture can make a great difference, showing the embroidery to best advantage. So, never scrimp on materials or time.

I am an inveterate hoarder of fabrics and trimmings. I usually buy fabric simply because I like it, and then it may be years before that particular piece gets put to use. But when it does, it will be just the bit I wanted – and I will have enjoyed its presence in the cupboard in the meantime. So

next time you are about to put that fabric remnant back on the shop counter, don't – you will have a use for it, but maybe not for a while. Enjoy buying it – and a larger cupboard if needs be.

Rather than limit the book to one embroidery technique, I have used three: cross stitch, crewelwork and canvaswork. Cross stitch is probably the most popular and the one which will be familiar to most stitchers. If you do not know how to work cross stitch, you can learn quite easily by following the instructions and the charts, and then referring to the photographs of the finished pieces. All the charts can be worked in the traditional way for canvaswork, that is in tent stitch on canvas, as well as cross stitch on evenweave fabrics. I have added another dimension to most of the canvaswork projects by combining canvaswork with simple crewelwork stitches. This technique makes the design stand out in relief against the flat background of tent stitch and I have called it 'woolwork'. In woolworking the stitches are not counted and so the designs have to be traced on to the canvas and then worked using the stitches from the crewelwork section, then the background is filled in with tent stitch and a counted border may be added.

Crewelwork is not quite as popular as cross stitch or canvaswork, this is because it has gained a reputation for being difficult, but this is not so. It is free form and non-counted, worked on smooth, non-evenweave fabric and like any other form of embroidery this is a technique you can learn. The Materials and Techniques section at the back of the book gives general information on how to work crewel embroidery, and the projects give more detailed instructions. Once you have the knack of crewelwork – it is almost like painting with yarn – you will be able to work designs without the need of step-by-step instructions.

For every flower I have given a chart for cross stitch and canvaswork and a coloured drawing for crewelwork and woolwork. I haven't given detailed instructions in each technique for each flower,

Zinnia cross stitch picture (top, see page 103) and
orange blossom canvaswork inset velvet pincushion
(bottom, see page 60).

however – once you've mastered a given technique you won't need full instructions. So if, for example, you haven't tried crewelwork before, I suggest that you start with the flower miniatures, which are small and have full instructions. Then move on to one of the larger flower pictures that also has full instructions. Eventually, try stitching one of the flowers for which there is either a drawing or chart but no instructions.

The charts, when stitched on 28-count evenweave or 14-count Aida, will be about the same size as the coloured line drawings. Of course, either can be altered: the charted stitching by using a different count fabric and the line drawings by enlarging or reducing on a photocopier. The threads used – stranded cotton (floss), both DMC and the Anchor equivalents, and Appleton crewel wool (yarn) – are listed on the charts. You will need one skein of each unless directed otherwise.

Do not stem your own creativity by sticking slavishly to my charts and drawings. For example, if you want to work something small, pick a detail from a larger design and use that. With the Rose Pincushion (see page 74) I suggest you use a tiny bit of the rose design and work it on a scrap of canvas. Back that with a lovely piece of velvet and fill with wadding (batting) and you have a beautiful, and useful, object. What you can do with the rose you can do with any other design in the book. Use different fabrics from the ones I suggest. Use different colourways. Mount flowers in the same way to create a set. The possibilities are almost endless; do try the different embroidery techniques. I really hope this book will be a starting point for you to try new techniques as well as an opportunity to continue the type of stitching you enjoy.

Finally, I have gathered the snippets of folklore and recipes from numerous sources to add interest to these pages and help you to choose the flower you are to embroider. However, I have not tested any of the recipes or cures (some of them I certainly would not want to) and accept no responsibility whatsoever for any strange things that may happen if you do!

Some of the projects featured in this book. From left: woolwork viola pincushion; woolwork polyanthus footstool; nasturtium canvaswork slipper; woolwork sunflower beaded pillow; named foldover purse and beaded ivy Christmas card.

ANEMONE

The anemone can be found in many different guises, from the delicate, white, wood anemone that grows wild in the woodlands in the spring to the vivid purple, blue and pink blossoms found in the florists' shops.

Forsaken

Woolwork Pillow

The rich colours seemed to ask for 'all the trimmings' – a dramatic black background, velvet, cords and tassels. These vivid shades will not blend into a subtle colour scheme – but then again, that is not in the nature of these impertinent blooms.

YOU WILL NEED

12in (30cm) square, 14-count interlock canvas
Appleton crewel wool (yarn) as listed
in the table on page 12
(3 skeins each are required of 896,
805 and 256, and 1 hank of 998 for background)
Size 22 tapestry needle
An embroidery frame
20in (50cm) velvet for making up

Stitches: Tent stitch, diagonal tent stitch, long legged cross stitch, long and short stitch, satin stitch, split backstitch, French knots
Thread: Use three strands of crewel wool (yarn) unless otherwise stated in the text

1 Enlarge the flower outline by 140% and trace on to your canvas (see page 115).
2 Mount the canvas into your frame if required (see page 114).
3 Read 'General Working Advice' (see page 116). The picture on this page and the chart on page 12 will help with placing the colours.
4 Begin stitching the purple flower on the right. Using light purple, work a row of long and short stitch around the outer edge of the petals leaving out the turned-over edges.
5 Work the next layer in dark purple, working from the centre of the flower outwards.
6 Work the turned-over parts of the petals in dark purple satin stitch. Complete the petals using ecru in the centre of the flower.
7 Fill the centre with black tent stitch and then cover this tent stitch with French knots. Randomly place a few French knots on the ecru part of the flower and join them to the centre with straight stitches. Placing French knots over tent stitch gives a padded effect to the flower centre and makes the knots sit better.

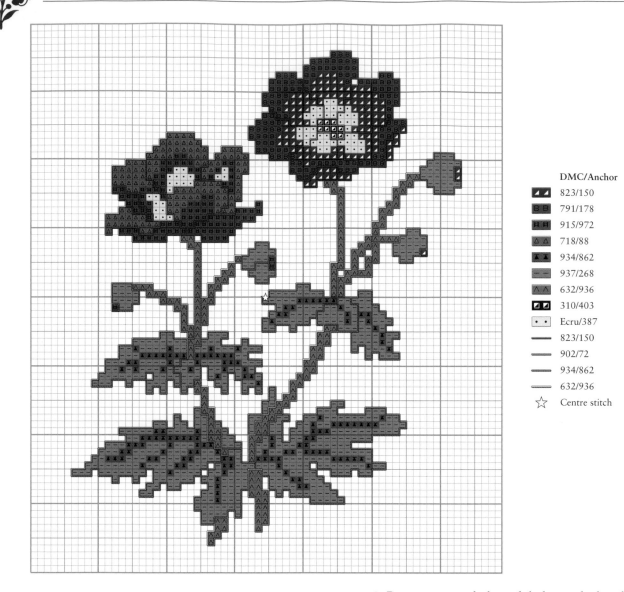

DMC/Anchor	
◢◢	823/150
B B	791/178
H H	915/972
△ △	718/88
▲ ▲	934/862
– –	937/268
∧ ∧	632/936
◨◨	310/403
• •	Ecru/387
——	823/150
——	902/72
——	934/862
——	632/936
☆	Centre stitch

ANEMONE

	DMC	Anchor	Appleton
Dark purple	823	150	106
Light purple	791	178	896
Dark pink	915	972	805
Light pink	718	88	803
Dark green	934	862	407
Light green	937	268	256
Brown	632	936	185
Black	310	403	993
Ecru	Ecru	387	992
French knots	310	403	993
Optional outlines			
Purple flower	823	150	852
Pink flower	902	72	716
Leaves	934	862	407
Stems	632	936	185

8 Repeat using dark and light pink for the other flower which has no middle but otherwise is worked in exactly the same way.

9 Work the leaves and buds in light green long and short stitch, adding a tip of colour to all the buds and dark green split backstitch veins to the leaves.

10 Work the stems in brown long and short stitch, beginning at the top of each stem and working down to the bottom. Add a few single stitches of light green using one strand of thread to add a colour variation.

11 Use the alphabet of your choice (see page 106) to add the name. Work the large 'A' in tent stitch, tucking it in under the lower leaf, and the rest of the word in backstitch letters once the background is completed.

12 Count a square that is 97 x 97 canvas threads to surround the design. Use pins to mark the square as you count so you can adjust to surround the flower. Allow the flower to cross this line in places where you need to – see the photograph on page 11. Your own design may differ slightly depending on how accurately the outline was enlarged. When you have decided on the correct placement, use a pencil to draw a line in the canvas groove that surrounds these 97 threads in each direction.

13 Work the background in black diagonal tent stitch taking care to tuck the stitches in under the long and short stitch of the design. Complete the word in backstitch if you are using it. Work a single row of light green tent stitch on the thread outside the background allowing it to break off where the lettering passes through. This green line is the inner line of the border.

14 Turn to page 110 for the twisted border pattern, and work in tent stitch from the chart in dark pink and light purple. Omit the outer line of the border and substitute a row of light green long legged cross stitch (see page 115) to complete and frame the panel.

15 When complete, stretch (see page 116), make the tassels and cords (see page 125) and make up (see page 121).

Cross Stitch Thread Folder

Use this pretty thread holder (pictured on page 33) to keep the threads for a current project, or make it much longer to hold your entire collection.

Design size: 5 x 4in (13 x 10cm)
Stitch count: 72 x 57

YOU WILL NEED

12 x 8in (30 x 20cm) 28-count cream linen
Stranded cotton (floss) as listed on the chart on page 12
Size 26 tapestry needle
9³/₄ x 30in (25 x 72cm) printed cotton fabric
2³/₄yd (2.5m) satin bias binding
10 x 18in (25 x 45cm) polyester wadding

Stitches: Cross stitch, backstitch, French knots
Threads: Use two strands of stranded cotton (floss) for the cross stitch and French knots, and one strand for the backstitch outline

1 Prepare your fabric (see page 112).
2 Following the chart on page 12 and starting at the centre, stitch the anemones. Scatter French knots in black on the ecru parts of each flower and on the petals near the centre – give some a straight stitch as a stalk. Work the word 'Threads' under the flowers, using the alphabet of your choice (see page 106).
3 When complete, press (see page 113).
4 To make up the thread folder, cut a piece of printed cotton 17 x 9in (43 x 23cm) and a piece of polyester wadding the same size. Cut two 17in (43cm) lengths of satin binding, fold them in half along the

length and top stitch the two edges together.
5 Lay the piece of printed cotton on the polyester wadding and then lay the two strips of binding along the length about 2in (5cm) from the edges and 4in (10cm) apart. Pin all this in place and then quilt lines dividing the length in half and half again until you have eight sections.
6 Trim the embroidered panel to 6 x 9in (15 x 23cm) and stitch to a piece of printed cotton 12 x 9in (30 x 23cm). Lay this panel on the back of the quilted piece already made and stitch together around the outer edge. Trim and bind the outer edge using the remaining satin binding.

Cross Stitch Lavender Bag

Adding a handmade scented sachet filled with lavender (pictured on page 4) to a covered hanger makes a more personal gift and only takes a short time to do. Buy the hanger or cover one yourself.

YOU WILL NEED

3in (8cm) square, cream 18-count Aida (or 36-count linen if you prefer)
Stranded cotton (floss) as listed on the chart on page 12 (no greens or brown)
Size 26 tapestry needle
12in (30cm) narrow ribbon and lace for trimming
A scrap of cotton fabric for backing

Stitches: Cross stitch, backstitch, French knots, long legged cross stitch
Threads: Use one strand of stranded cotton (floss) for the cross stitch, backstitch outline and French knots

1 Prepare your fabric (see page 112).
2 Following the chart on page 12, stitch the purple anemone flower head placing it centrally on the small square of fabric. Scatter French knots in black

Also called wind flower, because they

say the flowers never open but

when the wind blows.

Culpeper *The Complete Herbal*

on the ecru parts of the flower – give some a straight stitch as a stalk.

3 Work a square, 27 x 27 stitches, in light pink around the flower, then work a backstitch outline in dark pink on either side of the line.

4 Press (see page 113), and fold in the edges leaving four empty rows around the design. Trim away any excess fabric. Cut a square from the backing fabric to match the size of the design square.

5 Stitch the back to the front using long legged cross stitch in two strands of dark purple. Just before you sew up the edges, completely fill the little bag with lavender and then attach the ribbon to one corner. Trim the neck of the hanger with lace and tie on the lavender bag.

Crewel Miniature

The first in a set of five miniatures featured in this book. I traced the purple flower head from the coloured drawing and then moved the tracing around to add the tips of the lower leaves.

YOU WILL NEED

8in (20cm) square, fine linen union
Appleton crewel wool (yarn) as listed in the table on page 12 (except for brown)
Size 7 crewel needle
An embroidery hoop

'Youth, like a thin Anemone, displays

His silken leaf, and in a morn decays'

Rev H Friend *Flowers and Folklore Vol I*

Stitches: Long and short stitch, split backstitch and French knots
Thread: Use one strand of crewel wool (yarn) throughout

1 Prepare your fabric (see page 117); then trace the flower outline on to it (see page 117) and mount it into your hoop or frame (see page 117).

2 Read 'General Working Advice' (see page 119). The picture on page 10 and the chart on page 12 will help with placing the colours.

3 Begin with light purple and work a split backstitch outline to the four petals without turned-over edges.

4 Still using light purple, work a row of long and short stitch along the outer edge then work rows in dark purple and ecru to the middle of the flower. You may need to make two layers of ecru to fill the petals.

5 Outline the turned-over edges of the other two petals in split backstitch and work long and short stitch over in dark purple. Complete the petals in the same way as the first four.

6 Add randomly placed French knots in black towards the centre of the flower and a cluster of black French knots in the middle. Make small straight stitches joining some of the outer knots to the central cluster.

7 Outline the leaves in light green split backstitch, and fill with long and short stitch in light green. Work the veins in dark green split backstitch.

8 When complete, wash and press (see page 120). Mount and frame as required.

Anemone crewelwork miniature.

BLUEBELL

This lovely wild plant paints the countryside with an ethereal blue haze in springtime. Its fragrant, deep blue, almost violet blooms carpet our woodland floors; and visitors flock to see these enchanting bluebell woods.

Constancy

Cross Stitch Tea Cosy

Not very practical but terribly feminine! You will need to get your bone china out for this one.

Design size: 7 x 4¹/₂ in (18 x 11 cm)
Stitch count: 102 x 63

YOU WILL NEED

16 x 12in (40 x 30cm) 28-count ivory linen
Stranded cotton (floss) as listed on page 18
Size 26 tapestry needle
Fabric for backing – or use the same linen as the front, in which case you could embroider both sides of the tea cosy
2¹/₄yd (2m) lace for trimming
39in (1m) satin bias binding for the bottom edge
A tea cosy liner – old-fashioned haberdashers sell calico-covered, padded tea cosy liners. Or make one yourself out of calico and polyester wadding. It is a good idea to have a removable liner on such a light-coloured cosy

Tea cosy: I have not included measurements for the tea cosy because you will probably want it to fit a special teapot. Measure the pot in height and width and add on about 2in (5cm) in each dimension. As this is a dainty design it should be used for quite a small pot
Stitches: Cross stitch, backstitch, French knots
Threads: Use two strands of stranded cotton (floss) for the cross stitch and French knots, and one strand for the backstitch outline

1 Prepare your fabric (see page 112).
2 Following the chart on page 18 and starting at the centre, stitch the bluebell. Add one or two French knots in yellow to the centre of the end of each bell.
3 When complete, press (see page 113).
4 Lay the tea cosy liner carefully over the embroidery making sure that the flower is centrally placed. Cut out, allowing a ¹/₂in (1.25cm) seam allowance. Cut another from the backing fabric you have chosen.

15

5 Gather the lace to fit the edge and stitch on to the front panel right sides together with the lace edge inwards. Make a loop out of 2¹/₂in (6.5cm) of the satin binding and attach to the top edge in the middle.
6 Lay the back of the tea cosy over the front, right sides together with the lace between the two layers, and stitch along the same line as the one that attached the lace. Trim and oversew this seam and turn right sides out.
7 Try the shape over the liner and trim the bottom edge if necessary. Bind this edge with satin binding.

Cross Stitch Beaded Jug Cover

I remember being fascinated by one of these that my grandmother used in her conservatory to keep the wasps out of the lemonade.

YOU WILL NEED

10in (25cm) square, creamy white muslin
Stranded cotton (floss) as listed on the chart on page 18
Size 26 tapestry needle
Twelve glass beads, heavy enough to weight the cover

Stitches: Cross stitch, backstitch, French knots
Threads: Use two strands for the cross stitch and French knots, and one strand for the backstitch outline
Fabric: Muslin is very loosely woven and you will need to take care not to pull your stitches too tightly. Stitch over four threads for the cross stitch. Because muslin is not an evenweave fabric the stitching may be uneven

1 Prepare your fabric (see page 112).
2 Following the chart on page 18, stitch the buds and the next three bells on the flower stalk in the centre of the muslin. Add three yellow French knots in the centre of each open flower.
3 Find a plate that is about 8in (20cm) in diameter, place it over the bluebell, taking care to centre the flower, and draw round it with a soft pencil. Cut out and finish off the edge to prevent fraying – either zigzag on a sewing machine or oversew by hand.
4 Turn the edge over a little and oversew using three strands of mid hyacinth. When you reach the beginning again, reverse the direction of your stitching and oversew back the other way. This makes the cross stitch effect on the edge of the jug cover.
5 Attach twelve glass beads at the points of a clock around the edge of the circle.

Set a pretty table with this bluebell tea cosy and jug cover and daffodil jam pot cover and food umbrella.

Bluebell

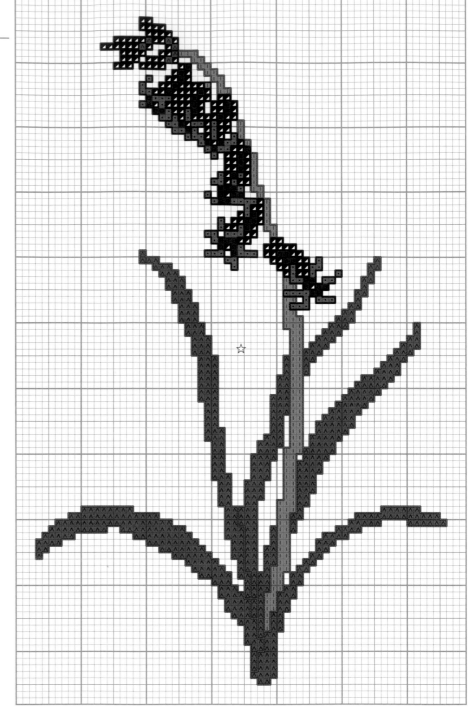

DMC/Anchor

◢◣	791/178
⋀ ⋀	792/177
⫼ ⫼	793/176
••	937/268
▦▦	470/266
—	823/150
—	937/268
☆	Centre stitch

BLUEBELL

	DMC	Anchor	Appleton
Dark hyacinth	791	178	896
Mid hyacinth	792	177	895
Light hyacinth	793	176	894
Dark green	937	268	256
Light green	470	266	254
French knots	783	307	474
Optional outlines			
Flowers	823	150	852
Leaves and stems	937	268	256

I love a lassie, a bonnie bonnie lassie,

She's as pure as the Lily in the dell,

She's as sweet as the heather –

The bonnie bloomin' heather –

Mary ma Scotch Bluebell.

Music hall song sung by Sir Harry Lauder

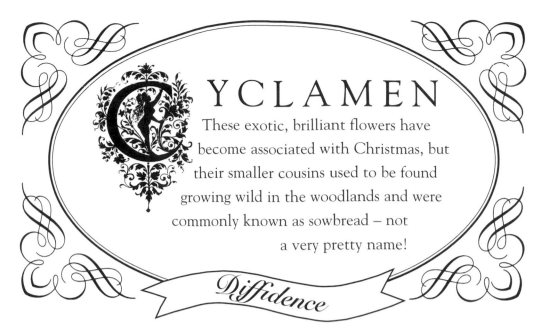

CYCLAMEN

These exotic, brilliant flowers have become associated with Christmas, but their smaller cousins used to be found growing wild in the woodlands and were commonly known as sowbread – not a very pretty name!

Diffidence

Cross Stitch Picture

If you decide to display your picture in a covered mount find a fabric that picks out the colours in the flower. Time taken to find a good match will be rewarded by the finished result.

Design size: 5 x 3½in (13 x 9cm)
Stitch count: 76 x 52

YOU WILL NEED

12in (30cm) square, 28-count cream linen
Stranded cotton (floss) as listed on the chart on page 20
Size 26 tapestry needle
12in (30cm) square, printed cotton fabric
8in (20cm) square, polyester wadding

Stitches: Cross stitch, backstitch
Threads: Use two strands of stranded cotton (floss)
for the cross stitch and one strand for the
backstitch outline

1 Prepare your fabric (see page 112).
2 Following the chart on page 20 and starting at the centre, stitch the cyclamen.
3 When complete, press (see page 113). Make a covered mount and trim with a bow made of the same fabric (see page 121). Frame as required.

Look under the leaves of dwarf cyclamen in your garden in July for little pods bursting with round, brown seeds. Harvest them before the mice eat them, plant in pots and grow on.

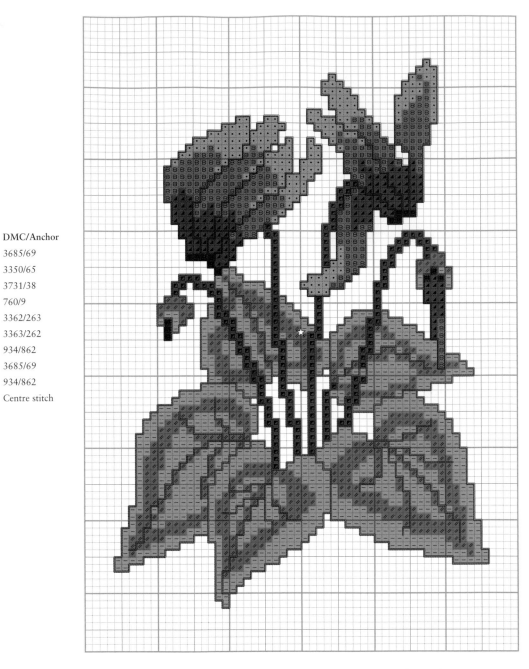

DMC/Anchor

■	3685/69
◢◣	3350/65
B B	3731/38
· ·	760/9
▨	3362/263
- -	3363/262
▨ ▨	934/862
——	3685/69
——	934/862
☆	Centre stitch

CYCLAMEN

	DMC	Anchor	Appleton
Dark pink	3685	69	805
Mid pink	3350	65	803
Light pink	3731	38	802
Lightest pink	760	9	801
Dark blue/green	3362	263	295
Light blue/green	3363	262	293
Green	934	862	407
Optional outlines			
Flowers	3685	69	805
Leaves and stems	934	862	407

Cyclamen, valued as a medicinal plant,

an aphrodisiac and an

antidote to poison, was also considered

to be a drinker's plant because

if a small amount was added to wine

it quickly resulted in drunkenness.

~

*Opposite: Cyclamen cross stitch picture and fritillary
etui and scissor keeper.*

DAFFODIL

Like the bluebell the daffodil is a protected species. It has declined drastically in the wild as people dig up the bulbs to plant in their gardens. A traditional symbol of spring, the daffodil is also the quintessential Easter flower.

Regard

Cross Stitch Food Umbrella

This must be the ideal present for somebody who has everything, because they are highly unlikely to have something like this! It is pictured on page 24.

Design size: 6¹/₂ x 3¹/₂in (16 x 9cm)
Stitch count: 93 x 48

YOU WILL NEED

10 x 8in (25 x 20cm) 28-count ivory linen
Stranded cotton (floss) as listed on the chart on page 23
Size 26 tapestry needle
39in (1m) lace for trimming
A purchased food umbrella

Umbrella: If you're not happy with the food umbrella you buy, dismantle it and use the discarded pieces as a pattern to re-cover it in cotton muslin. I cannot be more specific because it will depend on what your umbrella is like, but I can tell you that it was a much easier job than I expected
Stitches: Cross stitch, backstitch
Threads: Use two strands of stranded cotton (floss) for the cross stitch and one strand for the backstitch outline

The daffodil bulb has narcotic properties. It is a purgative in small doses and was recommended by Culpeper for use against all obstructions in the body.

DMC/Anchor

∧∧	470/266
••	725/306
B B	727/293
◢◢	977/313
✛✛	937/268
——	977/313
——	937/268
☆	Centre stitch

1 Prepare your fabric (see page 112).

2 Following the chart above and starting at the centre, stitch the daffodil.

3 When complete, press (see page 113).

4 Re-cover the umbrella if necessary.

5 Draw an oval measuring about 6 x 8in (15 x 20cm) to surround the embroidered daffodil. The easy way to do this is to find something to draw round, such as a picture frame.

6 Make a join in the lace and gather to fit the circumference of the oval. Stitch to the oval right sides together and then turn the seam under and carefully press this edge (try not to flatten the lace).

7 Pin the lace-edged oval to one side of the umbrella and topstitch in place.

DAFFODIL

	DMC	Anchor	Appleton
Light green	470	266	254
Dark yellow	725	306	473
Light yellow	727	293	471
Orange	977	313	862
Dark green	937	268	256
Optional outlines			
Flowers	977	313	862
Leaves and stems	937	268	256

Cross Stitch Jam Pot Cover

An ideal way of using up odd bits of linen, this would work equally well with most of the charted flowers in this book. Why not select other flowers and make a set? It is pictured on page 17.

Design size: 1¹/₂ x 2¹/₂in (4 x 6cm)

YOU WILL NEED

6in (15cm) square, 28-count ivory linen
Stranded cotton (floss) as listed on the chart on page 23
Size 26 tapestry needle
24in (60cm) lace for trimming
20in (50cm) narrow ribbon

Stitches: Cross stitch, backstitch
Threads: Use two strands of stranded cotton (floss) for the cross stitch and one strand for the backstitch outline

1 Prepare your fabric (see page 112).
2 Following the chart on page 23, stitch the daffodil on the left, some of the stem and a bit of the stem that lies next to it. The back petals of the flower should be central in your piece of fabric.
3 When complete, press (see page 113).

4 Draw a circle around the flower and oversew the edge, either by hand or zig-zag on a sewing machine.
5 Top stitch the lace on, gathering it slightly to make a circle. Pull it over the jar and fix with a rubber band. Tie the ribbon around to cover the band.
6 Now select bits of other charts and make a set!

I wandered lonely as a cloud

That floats on high o'er vales and hills,

When all at once I saw a crowd,

A host, of golden daffodils;

Beside the lake, beneath the trees,

Fluttering and dancing in the breeze

William Wordsworth *I wandered lonely as a cloud*

Daffodil cross stitch food umbrella.

EGLANTINE

I make no excuse for including the brightly-coloured eglantine as well as the pale dog rose – truly old roses that both deserve places in this alphabet of flowers. What could be more delightful than a hedge bedecked with these bright blooms?

I wound to heal

Cross Stitch Picture

A bow decorating a small picture (pictured on page 33) makes an enchanting effect. Match the fabric to the colours in the embroidery or alternatively to the decor of your room.

Design size. 4¹/₂ x 4¹/₂in (12 x 12cm)
Stitch count: 68 x 69

YOU WILL NEED

10in (25cm) square, 28-count cream linen
Stranded cotton (floss) as listed on the chart on page 26
Size 26 tapestry needle

Stitches: Cross stitch, backstitch
Threads: Use two strands of stranded cotton (floss) for the cross stitch and one strand for the backstitch outline

1 Prepare your fabric (see page 112).
2 Following the chart on page 26 and starting at the centre, stitch the eglantine. The lines at the top of the hip are straight stitches in one strand of brown.
3 When complete, press (see page 113). Mount and frame as required. To make a ribbon and bow hanger see page 121.

Also known as sweet briar, they were popular plants in medieval gardens because of their sweetly aromatic leaves, which smell of apples, especially after rain.

25

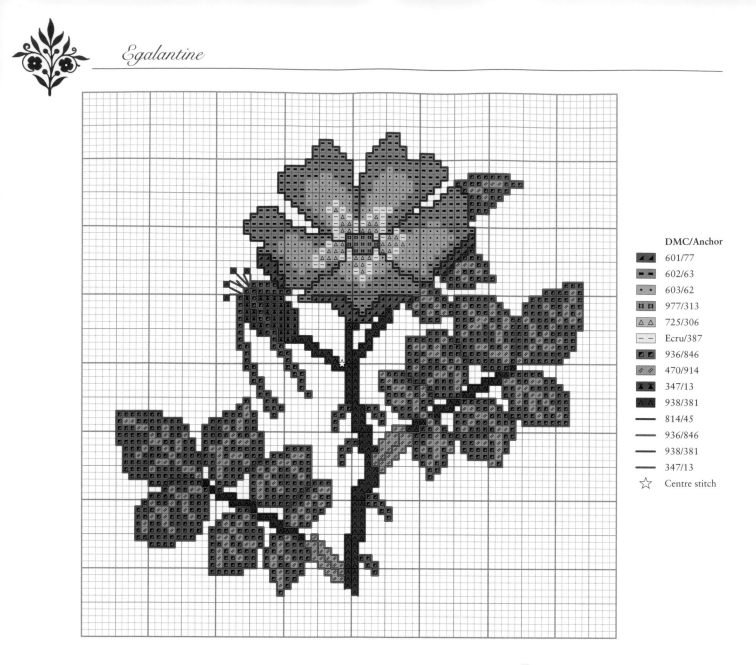

	DMC	Anchor
◢◢	601/77	
▬▬	602/63	
· ·	603/62	
H H	977/313	
△ △	725/306	
– –	Ecru/387	
◪ ▨	936/846	
◨ ◨	470/914	
▲ ▲	347/13	
◣ ◣	938/381	
—	814/45	
—	936/846	
—	938/381	
—	347/13	
☆	Centre stitch	

I know a bank whereon the wild thyme blows,

Where oxlips and the nodding violet grows

Quite over-canopied with luscious woodbine,

With sweet musk-roses, and with eglantine.

Shakespeare *A Midsummer Night's Dream*

EGLANTINE

	DMC	Anchor	Appleton
Dark pink	601	77	947
Mid pink	602	63	945
Light pink	603	62	944
Orange	977	313	862
Yellow	725	306	473
Ecru	Ecru	387	992
Dark green	936	846	256
Light green	470	914	254
Red	347	13	504
Brown	938	381	957
Optional outlines			
Flower	814	45	148
Leaves	936	846	256
Stems	938	381	957
Rosehip	347	13	504

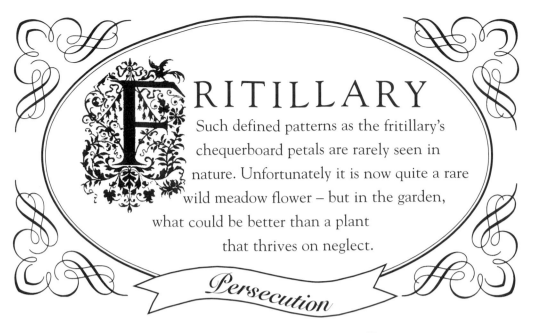

FRITILLARY

Such defined patterns as the fritillary's chequerboard petals are rarely seen in nature. Unfortunately it is now quite a rare wild meadow flower – but in the garden, what could be better than a plant that thrives on neglect.

Persecution

Victorian Etui

These pretty little folding boxes (pictured on page 28) often held Victorian ladies' sewing accessories. Rather than make your own, use one of the several kits that are available.

Design size. 5 x 5in (13 x 13cm)
Stitch count: 74 x 70

YOU WILL NEED

For the cross stitch panel
12in (30cm) square, 8-count cream linen
Stranded cotton (floss) as listed on the chart on page 29
Size 26 tapestry needle

For the crewelwork panel
12in (30cm) square, fine cream linen union
Stranded cotton (floss) as above
Size 7 crewel needle
An embroidery hoop or small frame

A kit for making the box (see Suppliers, page 126)
Fabric, wadding, ribbons, glue etc for
making up (follow kit instructions for quantities)

Latin name *Fritillaria* – a fritillaria was a small, bell-shaped container made of leather carried by Roman soldiers to contain and shake their gaming dice. The shape of these leather dice shakers made of panels of coloured leather gave the name to the chequered fritillary flower with its distinctive bell shape.

CROSS STITCH PANEL

Stitches: Cross stitch, backstitch
Threads: Use two strands of stranded cotton (floss)
for the cross stitch and one strand for the
backstitch outline

1 Prepare your fabric (see page 112).
2 Following the chart on page 29 and starting at the centre, stitch the fritillary.
3 When complete, press (see page 113).

CREWELWORK PANEL

Stitches: Long and short stitch, split backstitch,
French knots
Threads: Use three stands of stranded cotton (floss) for
the long and short stitch and French knots, and one
strand for the split backstitch.

1 Prepare your fabric (see page 117); then trace on to it the flower on the left of the drawing and the leaf above it with a short piece of stem (see page 117); and mount it into your hoop or frame
2 Read 'General Working Advice' (see page 119). The picture on page 27 and the chart on page 29 will help with placing the colours.
3 Using dark and light mauve, work the petals in long and short stitch. You will find it helps to work one petal at a time and keep two needles going at the same time, one threaded with each colour, to achieve the chequered effect. The two outer petals are nearly all dark except for a touch of light at the tip.
4 Outline the petals in dark blue split backstitch and add the petal mid lines using the drawing to help you to place them. Add a cluster of yellow French knots between the middle petals.

Fritillary Victorian etui.

5 Work the stem and leaf in long and short stitch beginning at the tip of the leaf and the flower head.
6 When complete, wash (see page 120) and press (see page 120).
7 If you like, add a ribbon trim to the two embroidered panels, framing the embroideries. Then make up the box according to the manufacturer's instructions, using the panels for the top and the inside bottom. One word of warning: this box takes a long time to make and you need to be extremely accurate with the cutting, sticking and stitching. Do not try to hurry it because you will surely spoil it!

Cross Stitch Scissor Keeper

This little object is quick to do and makes a delightful gift. Use the alphabet of your choice, shown at the back of the book, to add a friend's initials to make a really personal present.

YOU WILL NEED

8 x 4in (20 x 10cm) 28-count natural linen
Stranded cotton (floss) as listed on the chart on page 29
Size 26 tapestry needle
A small amount of polyester wadding for filling

Stitches: Cross stitch, backstitch, long legged
cross stitch
Threads: Use two strands of stranded cotton (floss) for
the cross stitch and long legged cross stitch, and one
strand for the backstitch outline

1 Prepare your fabric (see page 112). Fold in half, press lightly and mark the fold with a line of tacking (basting) stitches. This line separates the back and the front of the scissor keeper.
2 Following the chart on page 29, stitch the flower on the left. Place the flower in the centre of one side of the linen and then add some stem and two leaves.
3 Work two rows of backstitch in dark green to surround the design with a square, allowing the design to break into the square in places.
4 Repeat the design on the other side of the piece of linen or personalize your scissor keeper with initials using the alphabet of your choice (see page 106).
5 When complete, press (see page 113).
6 To make up, fold in half down the centre line already marked. Then fold in the three edges so that the surround to the design is equal all the way around, and trim away any excess.
7 Make a twisted cord from some of the left-over threads (see page 125).

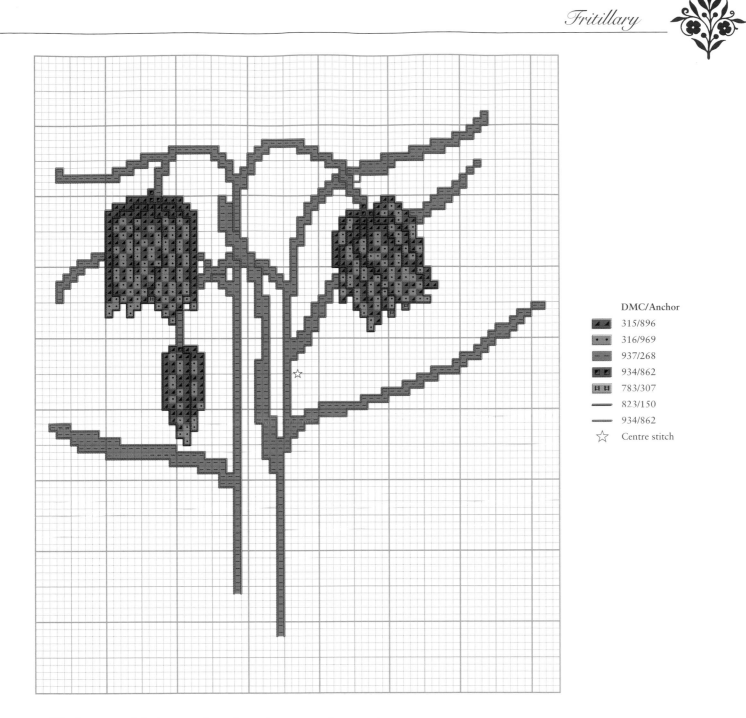

	DMC/Anchor
◢◢	315/896
••	316/969
	937/268
◪◪	934/862
H H	783/307
——	823/150
——	934/862
☆	Centre stitch

8 Work a row of dark green long legged cross stitch on the four middle threads (two either side of the centre line). This long legged cross stitch is worked over four threads across and progresses backwards and forwards two threads at a time. When you reach the corner, carry on with the long legged cross stitch by taking two linen threads from each folded-over edge. As you make this seam tuck in the two knotted ends of the cord at the corner at the top left of the fritillary.

9 Before you complete the sewing, fill well with polyester wadding.

10 To attach to your scissors, pass the loop through one handle and then put the keeper though the loop and pull tight.

FRITILLARY

	DMC	Anchor	Appleton
Dark mauve	315	896	714
Light mauve	316	969	711
Light green	937	268	256
Dark green	934	862	407
Yellow	783	307	474
Optional outlines			
Flower	823	150	852
Leaves and stems	934	862	407

GERANIUM

Probably discovered by Charles I's gardener Tradescant, the scented-leaved geraniums or pelargoniums are remarkable for their diversity. Some smell of roses, some of spices, some of peppermint or apples. They are much used in perfumery.

Comforting

Crewelwork Picture

When you've stitched this picture, why not make a set by working the polyanthus and viola crewelwork pictures (see pages 62 and 88) and framing them to match, see them all on page 91.

YOU WILL NEED

10in (25cm) square, fine linen union
Appleton crewel wool (yarn) as listed in the table on page 34
Size 7 crewel needle
An embroidery hoop or frame

Stitches: Long and short stitch, stem stitch, split backstitch and French knots
Threads: Use one strand of crewel wool (yarn) throughout

1 Prepare your fabric (see page 117); then trace the flower outline on to it (see page 117) and mount it in to your hoop or frame
2 Read 'General Working Advice' (see page 119). The picture on this page and the chart on page 34 will help with placing the colours.
3 Work a row of light green split backstitch around the edge of the leaves.

RECIPE FOR ROSE GERANIUM PUNCH

1¹/₂ pint (1 litre) apple juice

Four limes

8oz (200g) sugar

Six leaves rose-scented geranium

Boil the apple juice, sugar and leaves
for five minutes. Add thinly sliced and
crushed limes. Cool and strain on to ice in
tall glasses and garnish with geranium petals.

Geranium crewelwork picture.

4 Still using light green, work a row of long and short stitch along the outer edge of each leaf, then a row of dark green. Take care that the dark green row follows the outer shape of the leaf and that all the stitches radiate out from the centre. Work a last row of light green from the centre.

5 Work the veins in dark green split backstitch.

6 Work the stems as three close parallel lines of stem stitch in dark green.

7 Work each flower separately, completing one before starting another. All the stitches should radiate out from the centre of the flower. Begin at the outer edge of each flower in dark red long and short stitch; come up on the outer edge and down towards the centre. Work light red towards the centre of the

RECIPE FOR ROSE GERANIUM BUTTER

Butter pounded with the leaves makes a

delicious spread for cakes and biscuits when

topped with apple jelly.

Mrs Beeton

flower; come up at the centre and down through the dark red stitches, blending the colours.

8 Using dark green, make a single stitch between each petal and place a single French knot in the centre of each flower.

9 Finally, work the little buds in dark red and dark green (a few small stitches of each), and the stems to the little buds in dark green stem stitch.

10 When complete, wash and press (see page 120). Mount and frame as required.

Cross Stitch Workbag

What a great shame it is to carry beautiful handwork around in a nasty old plastic bag! If you are one of the culprits, here is how to do something about it.

Design size: 5¹/₂ x 3¹/₂in (14 x 9cm)
Stitch count: 66 x 51

YOU WILL NEED

10 x 8in (25 x 20cm) 28-count cream linen
Stranded cotton (floss) as listed on the chart on page 34
Size 26 tapestry needle
20in (50cm) printed cotton fabric (I used remnants of Liberty lawn, stitching strips together to give a patchwork effect and to make a piece large enough to make the bag)
20in (50cm) plain cotton or calico for lining
A pair of bag handles

Stitches: Cross stitch, backstitch, French knots
Threads: Use two strands of stranded cotton (floss) for the cross stitch and French knots, and one strand for the backstitch outline

1 Prepare your fabric (see page 112).

2 Following the chart on page 34 and starting at the centre, stitch the geranium. Add three French knots in light red to the green cross stitches that make the little buds that hang below the flower head.

3 Use the alphabet of your choice (see page 106) to add the flower name.

4 When complete, press (see page 113).

5 Using your chosen printed fabric, make a bag that is about one and a half times as wide as the handles. Either top stitch the embroidery on to it or inset it into the panels as you prefer. Line with plain cotton or calico, adding a pocket in the lining to hold your scissors and packets of needles. Gather the top and attach to your handles.

Clockwise from top left: Anemone cross stitch lavender bag, geranium cross stitch panel workbag, eglantine cross stitch picture and anemone quilted thread folder.

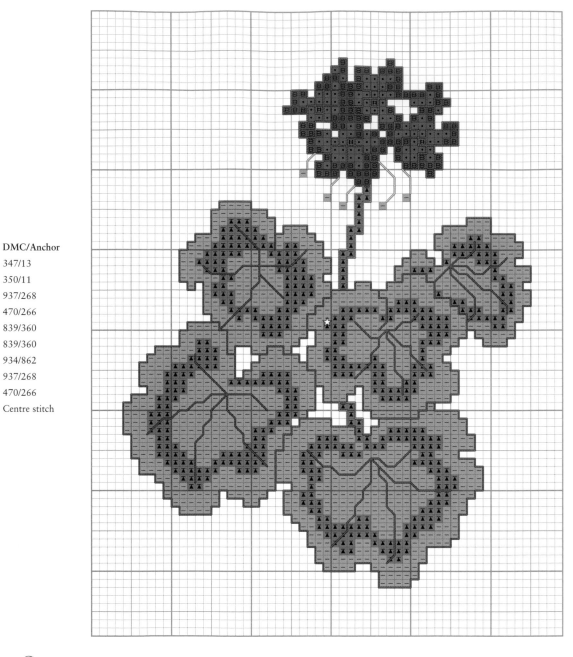

DMC/Anchor	
⊞ ⊞	347/13
• •	350/11
▲ ▲	937/268
– –	470/266
н н	839/360
——	839/360
——	934/862
——	937/268
——	470/266
☆	Centre stitch

GERANIUM

	DMC	Anchor	Appleton
Dark red	347	13	866
Light red	350	11	864
Dark green	937	268	244
Light green	470	266	242
Brown	839	360	956
Optional outlines			
Flower	839	360	956
Leaves	934	862	407
Stems	937	268	244
Bud stems	470	266	242

Sweet-scented geranium leaves have

a remarkable affinity with blackberries,

a few leaves added to the berries

when cooked with sugar add a

lovely flavour – especially when served

with clotted cream!

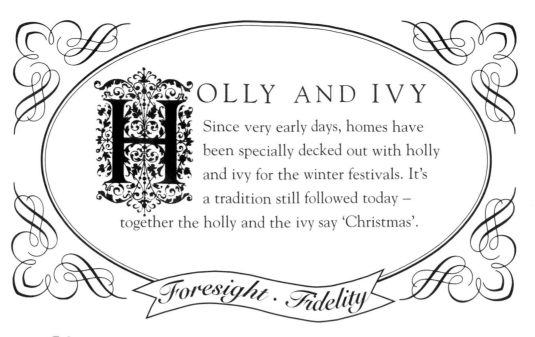

HOLLY AND IVY

Since very early days, homes have been specially decked out with holly and ivy for the winter festivals. It's a tradition still followed today – together the holly and the ivy say 'Christmas'.

Foresight · Fidelity

Christmas Treasure Box

Each year at Christmas, add another little treasure to the collection in the box. Silver thimbles, coins, jewels – the value can be real or sentimental.

Design size: Holly – 5 x 3½in (13 x 9cm); Ivy – 3 x 5in (8 x 13cm); together – approximately 8½ x 5in (21.5 x 12.5cm). This will vary, depending on the size of

your box lid and the length of the name. To work out the correct position of each element, mark the limits of the area to be stitched on squared paper, then add the name and birth date using the charts on pages 107 and 108. Draw in the outlines of the holly and ivy charts, arranged to fit in the space.

Stitch count: Holly 67 x 47; Ivy 39 x 71

YOU WILL NEED

14 x 12in (36 x 30cm) 28-count deep cream linen – this will depend on the size of your box lid
Stranded cotton (floss) as listed on the charts on pages 36 and 39
Size 26 tapestry needle
Wooden box – see Suppliers, page 126

Stitches: Cross stitch, backstitch
Threads: Use two strands of stranded cotton (floss) for the cross stitch and one strand for the backstitch outline

1 Prepare your fabric (see page 112).
2 Following the chart on page 36, work the holly on the left-hand half of the fabric about 1in (2.5cm) away from the centre line. Following the chart on page 39, work the ivy. How much you tuck it in under the holly will depend on the name that you want to include. In the design, as shown on page 37, the stem of the ivy begins three stitches to the right of the end stitch of the middle prickle of the bottom holly leaf. If your name is long you may need to adjust this; use the alphabets on pages 107 and 108.
3 Finally, work the name in dark red outlined in dark green, and the date below it in light green also outlined in dark green.
4 When complete, press (see page 113) and refer to the manufacturer's instructions for fitting to the box.
5 To make it really special, finish with a silk quilted lining and add piping to match around the edge of the box top.

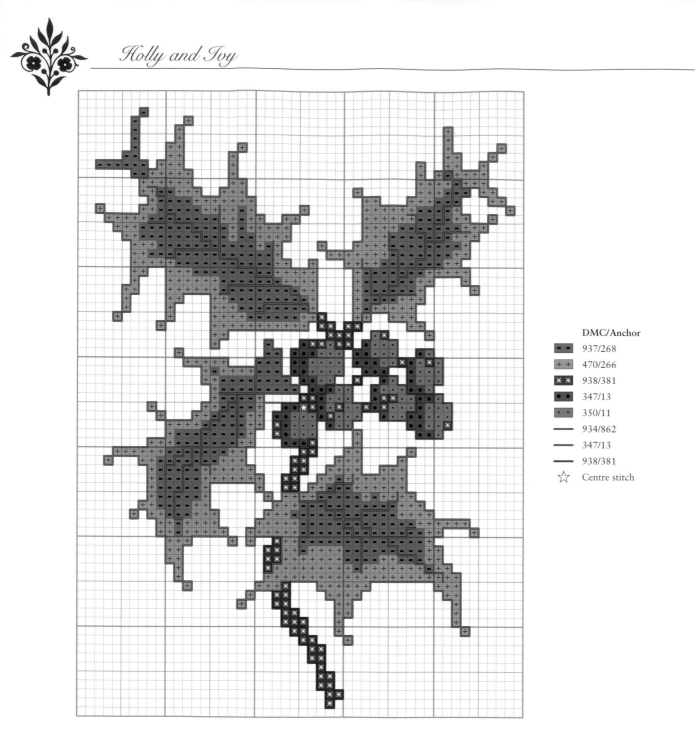

DMC/Anchor

■ ■	937/268
+ +	470/266
✹ ✹	938/381
● ●	347/13
· ·	350/11
——	934/862
——	347/13
——	938/381
☆	Centre stitch

HOLLY

	DMC	Anchor	Appleton
Dark green	937	268	256
Light green	470	266	254
Brown	938	381	187
Dark red	347	13	504
Light red	350	11	865
Optional outlines			
Leaves	934	862	407
Berries	347	13	504
Stem	938	381	187

The holly and the ivy,

When they are both full grown,

Of all the trees that are in the wood,

The holly bears the crown.

Opposite: Christmas treasure box (top) and holly and ivy Christmas cards.

Cross Stitch Christmas Cards

Never send cards in just a bare mount! Dress them up and make them really different; something special to be proud of.

HOLLY CARD

Perforated paper was very popular in Victorian times for making bookmarks, notebook covers and greetings cards. The designs were often of a religious nature and very intricate.

YOU WILL NEED

A sheet of stitching paper
Stranded cotton (floss) as listed on the chart on page 36
Size 26 tapestry needle
A card mount
A scrap of red silk dupion
Some sticky fixing pads
All-purpose clear adhesive
Antique gold spray paint
Paper doilies

Stitches: Cross stitch, backstitch
Threads: Use three strands for the cross stitch and two for the backstitch outline

1 Decide which leaves and berries you are going to use and stitch them next to each other on the paper, leaving enough space between to cut them out. The paper is surprisingly strong but you need to stitch by stabbing from one side of the paper to the other and not making stitches in one movement from the front of the work.
2 Use the alphabet of your choice (see page 106) to add your message.
3 When complete, cut out all the pieces using small, sharp scissors, leaving one row all around the design.
4 Line the card mount with red silk. Cut out bits of paper doily and spray with gold paint.
5 Arrange all the pieces carefully on the card mount and when you are sure that you are happy with the composition, start to glue. Use the sticky pads to attach the leaves and berries so they will stand out in relief from the rest of the card.

Holly is used to treat feelings of

hatred, envy and jealousy.

Dr Edward Bach *Bach Flower Remedies*

IVY CARD

Beadwork, another very popular form of needlework in Victorian times, brings the ivy design to life.

YOU WILL NEED

A scrap of 28-count natural linen
Mill Hill seed beads as listed in the table on page 39
Beige sewing thread
Stranded cotton (floss) for outlining
A beading needle
Size 26 tapestry needle
A card mount
All-purpose clear adhesive
Polyester wadding (batting)
Antique gold spray paint
Some dry leaves
Florist's paper ribbon

Stitches: Half cross stitch, backstitch
Threads: Use sewing thread for beading, and two strands of stranded cotton for the backstitch outline

1 Prepare your fabric (see page 112).
2 This design has been modified a little to suit beadwork. Outlining is not effective in amongst the beads

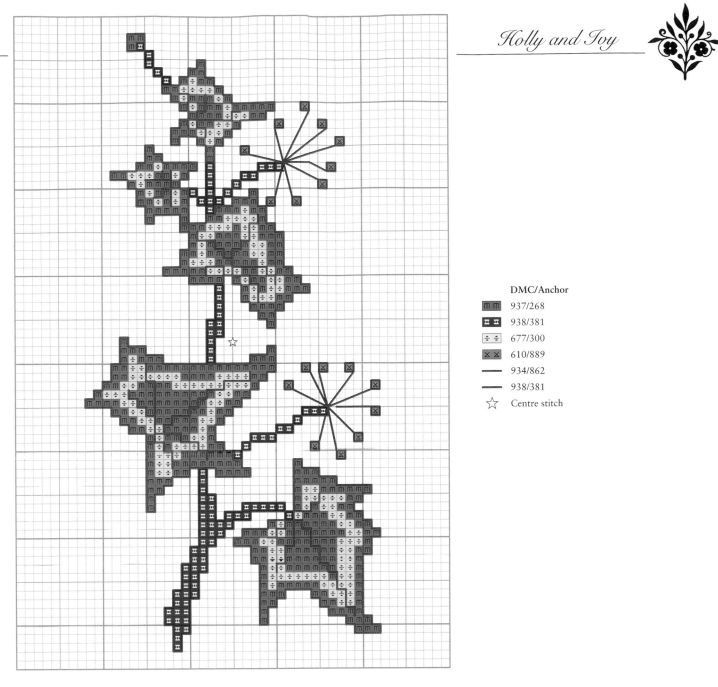

DMC/Anchor

▥ ▥	937/268
ᴤ ᴤ	938/381
÷ ÷	677/300
✕ ✕	610/889
—	934/862
—	938/381
☆	Centre stitch

so instead dark green beads should be stitched on to follow the dark green lines of the veins on the leaves. Use the same brown beads for the seed heads as for the stem. Decide how much of the chart you want to stitch. Thread the beading needle with sewing thread and follow the chart bearing in mind that you are using beads to make the veins of the leaves, working in half cross stitch and attaching a bead with each stitch (see page 120) where required. Outline in stranded cotton (floss).

3 Mount into the card, adding a layer of wadding (batting) under the beaded ivy.

4 Make up a bow from the florist's paper ribbon and spray this and the leaves with gold paint. Arrange all the pieces carefully and when you are sure that you are happy with the composition, start to glue.

IVY

	DMC	Anchor	Appleton
Green	937	268	256
Dark brown	938	381	187
Very pale gold	677	300	692
Light brown	610	889	954
Optional outlines			
Leaves	934	862	407
Stems and seedheads	938	381	187

Mill Hill seed beads
Green 00167
Dark brown 00330
Very pale gold 00123
Leaves 02020

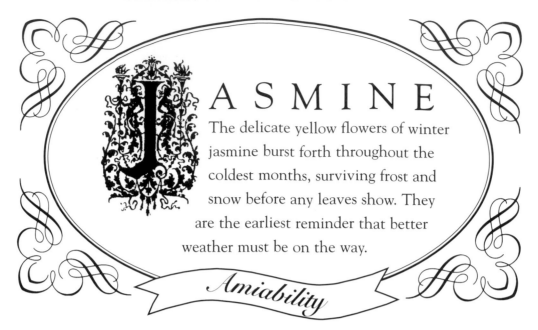

JASMINE

The delicate yellow flowers of winter jasmine burst forth throughout the coldest months, surviving frost and snow before any leaves show. They are the earliest reminder that better weather must be on the way.

Amiability

Cross Stitch Pillow

Even though the fabric used for this cushion was only a page out of a sample book, it went so well with the jasmine cross stitch that I had to use it! Backed with rust velvet, it makes a perfect tiny cushion.

Design size: 4¹/₂ x 3in (11 x 8cm)
Stitch count: 64 x 40

YOU WILL NEED

8in (20cm) square, 28-count cream linen
Stranded cotton (floss) as listed on the chart on page 41
Size 26 tapestry needle
10 x 12in (25 x 30cm) fabric for making up
10in (25cm) square for backing

Stitches: Cross stitch, backstitch
Threads: Use two strands of stranded cotton (floss) for the cross stitch and one strand for the backstitch outline

1 Prepare your fabric (see page 112).
2 Following the chart on page 41 and starting at the centre, stitch the jasmine.
3 When complete, press (see page 113), make tassels and cords (see page 125) and make up (see page 121).

Jasmine tea is a combination of fine China tea and aromatic jasmine flowers. With a pale colour and smooth light taste, its delicate floral flavour makes a most refreshing drink. It relieves colic and all sorts of digestive complaints.

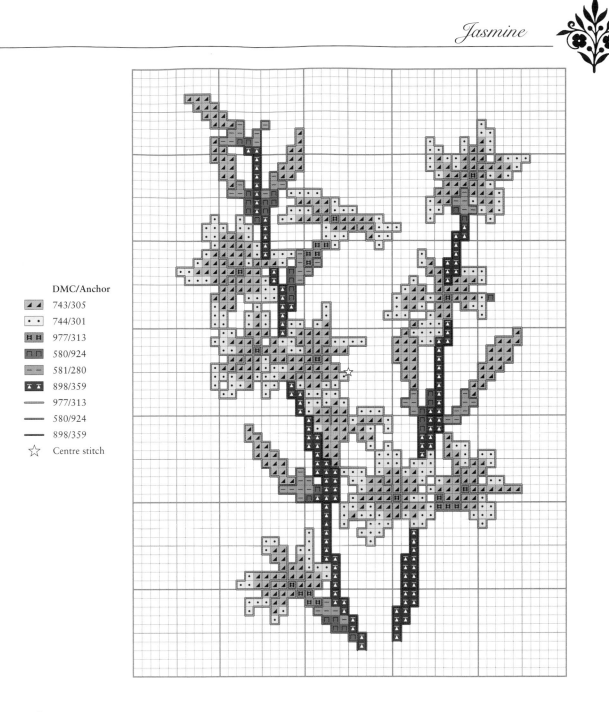

DMC/Anchor

▲▲	743/305
• •	744/301
⊞ ⊞	977/313
⊓ ⊓	580/924
— —	581/280
▲▲	898/359
—	977/313
—	580/924
—	898/359
☆	Centre stitch

JASMINE

	DMC	Anchor	Appleton
Dark yellow	743	305	473
Light yellow	744	301	471
Orange	977	313	862
Dark green	580	924	244
Light green	581	280	242
Brown	898	359	186
Optional outlines			
Flowers	977	313	862
Leaves	580	924	244
Stems	898	359	186

Jasmine perfume has always been
considered slightly aphrodisiac, and the
flowers were sometimes included
in love potions.

Winter jasmine is one of the most
tolerant and beautiful of
winter-flowering shrubs. A wall shrub, it
will thrive whatever the aspect
– sunny or not – producing
bright yellow flowers on bare
branches from early winter through
to spring. It comes
from Western China and was
introduced into this country in 1844 by
the botanist Robert Fortune.

The square root of half a number of bees,
and also eight-ninths of the whole,
alighted on the jasmines,
and a female buzzed responsive to the hum of the
male inclosed at night in a water-lily.

Longfellow *Kavanagh*

Striking jasmine cross stitch panel pillow.

KINGCUP

Kingcups – or marsh marigolds – can be found in early spring lighting up marshlands and damp woods. The brilliant golden flowers continue well into summer, and if you have a pond in your garden they will attract numerous insects.

Desire of riches

Beaded Cross Stitch Picture

This common wild flower looks very rich when stitched on deep red evenweave. Alternatively, try black for a similarly exotic effect.

Design size: 5½ x 4in (14 x 10cm)
Stitch count: 75 x 52

YOU WILL NEED

12 x 10in (30 x 25cm) 28-count deep red evenweave
Stranded cotton (floss) as listed on the chart on page 46
Size 26 tapestry needle
Mill Hill seed beads as listed in the table on page 46
A beading needle
Green sewing thread

Stitches: Cross stitch, backstitch, French knots
Threads: Use two strands of stranded cotton (floss) for the cross stitch, one strand for the backstitch outline, and sewing thread for beading

1 Prepare your fabric (see page 112).
2 Following the chart on page 46 and starting at the centre, stitch the kingcup.
3 To fill in the centres of the flowers, thread the beading needle with the sewing thread and follow the chart, working in half cross stitch and attaching a bead with each stitch (see page 120). Alternatively, fill the centre with a tightly packed cluster of French knots. Use the alphabet of your choice (see page 106) to add the name.
4 When complete, press (see page 113). Mount and frame as required.

In many parts of the British Isles farmers would hang kingcups over the byres of their cows on May Day to protect them from evil fairies and witches.

Opposite: Kingcup (top) and lily of the valley (bottom) beaded cross stitch pictures.

Kingcup

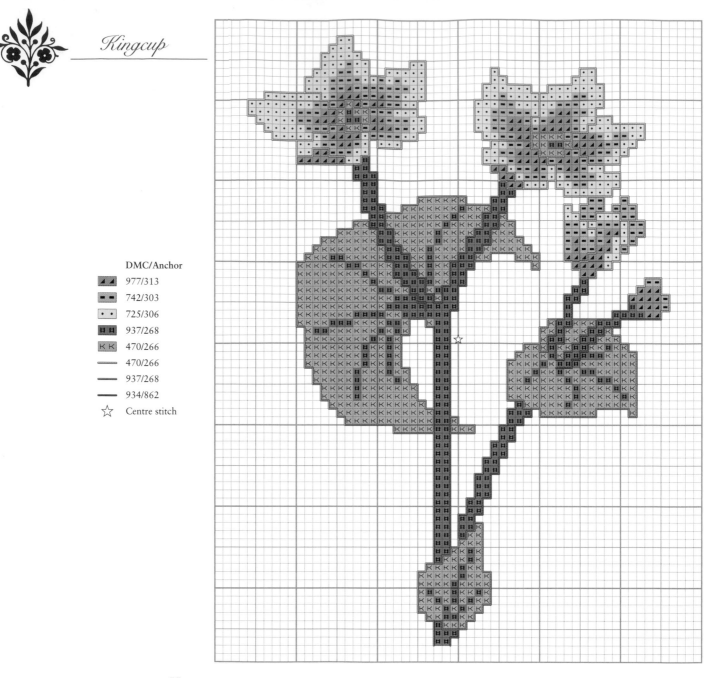

DMC/Anchor

◤◤	977/313
▪▪	742/303
∙∙	725/306
Ħ Ħ	937/268
ĸ ĸ	470/266
———	470/266
———	937/268
———	934/862
☆	Centre stitch

KINGCUP

	DMC	Anchor	Appleton
Orange	977	313	862
Dark yellow	742	303	474
Light yellow	725	306	472
Dark green	937	268	244
Light green	470	266	242
Optional outlines			
Flowers	470	266	242
Leaves	937	268	244
Stems	934	862	407

Mill Hill seed beads
Dark green 02020
Light green 00167

The single variety of kingcup was one
of the favourite plants of Gertrude Jekyll,
the queen of Victorian gardening.

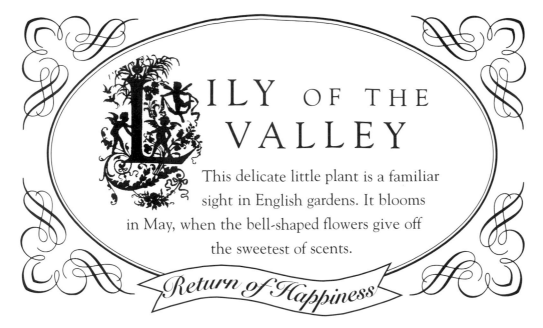

LILY OF THE VALLEY

This delicate little plant is a familiar
sight in English gardens. It blooms
in May, when the bell-shaped flowers give off
the sweetest of scents.

Return of Happiness

Beaded Cross Stitch Picture

Pearly white beads for the flowers, sewn on the same
dark red evenweave as the kingcup makes a delightful pair of pictures. They are pictured on page 45.

Design size: 5 x 3in (13 x 8cm)
Stitch count: 67 x 43

YOU WILL NEED

12 x 10in (30 x 25cm) 28-count deep red evenweave
Stranded cotton (floss) as listed on the chart on page 48
Size 26 tapestry needle
Mill Hill seed beads as listed in the table on page 48
A beading needle
Cream sewing thread

Stitches: Cross stitch, backstitch, French knots
Threads: Use two strands of stranded cotton (floss) for
the cross stitch, one strand for the backstitch outline,
and sewing thread for the beading

1 Prepare your fabric (see page 112).
2 Following the chart on page 48 and starting at the
centre, first stitch all the leaves and stems of the
lily of the valley.
3 To work the flowers, thread the beading needle
with sewing thread and follow the chart, working in
half cross stitch and attaching a bead with each stitch
(see page 120). Alternatively, work the flowers in
cross stitch in ecru stranded cotton.
4 Outline in stranded cotton if desired, and add a
gold French knot to some of the flowers. Use the
alphabet of your choice (see page 106) to add the
name.
5 When complete, press (see page 113). Mount and
frame as required.

It is said, in Devon, that lily of

the valley is an unlucky plant and anyone

who plants a bed of lily of the valley

will be dead within the year!

47

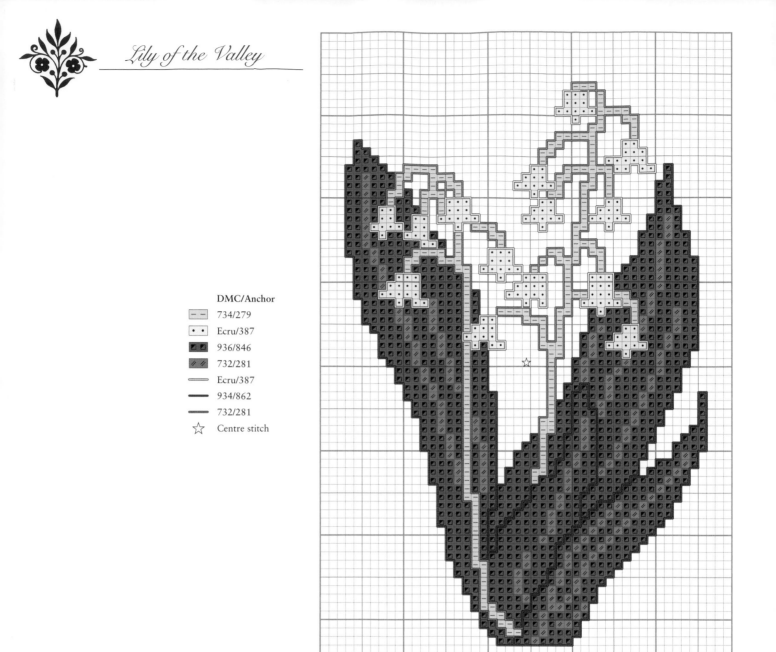

DMC/Anchor

− − −	734/279
• • •	Ecru/387
■ ■	936/846
⫽ ⫽	732/281
———	Ecru/387
———	934/862
———	732/281
☆	Centre stitch

LILY OF THE VALLEY

	DMC	Anchor	Appleton
Light green	734	279	333
Ecru	Ecru	387	992
Dark green	936	846	336
Mid green	732	281	334
French knots	977	313	862
Optional outlines			
Flowers	Ecru	387	992
Leaves	934	862	407
Stems	732	281	334

Mill Hill seed beads
Ecru 00123

Strengthens the brain, recruits a weak

memory and makes it strong again!

———

Culpeper

MAGNOLIA

The large, exotic flowers of the beautiful magnolia look almost as if they're made of porcelain – surely they would be happier in warmer climes. In fact magnolia thrives in Britain, and needs little attention.

Love of nature

Cross Stitch Picture

Capturing the seemingly fragile delicacy of the magnolia flower, with its soft, pale colours, this small framed picture would fit happily into almost any colour scheme.

Design size: 4¹/₂ x 3in (11 x 8cm)
Stitch count: 58 x 37

YOU WILL NEED

10in (25cm) square, 28-count natural linen
Stranded cotton (floss) as listed on the chart on page 52
Size 26 tapestry needle

Stitches: Cross stitch, backstitch
Threads: Use two strands of stranded cotton (floss) for the cross stitch and one strand for the backstitch outline

1 Prepare your fabric (see page 112).
2 Following the chart on page 52 and starting at the centre, stitch the magnolia.
3 Use the alphabet of your choice (see page 106) to add the name.
4 When complete, press (see page 113). Mount and frame as required.

Magnolia is an important plant
in ancient Chinese and American Indian
medicine, the bark being used in both
cultures to cure coughs and colds.

In addition to its use as a medicine,
the buds of the Yulan,
a Chinese species of magnolia,
was used for flavouring rice dishes.

Tea made from the bark of magnolia is
said to break the tobacco habit.

Handkerchief Purse

Not just for handkerchieves – this purse could hold
special pieces of jewellery, particularly suitable when
you travel. It would make a beautiful gift.

YOU WILL NEED

10 x 8in (25 x 20cm) fine linen
Appleton crewel wool (yarn) as listed in the table on
page 52
Size 7 crewel needle
An embroidery hoop or frame
20in (50cm) cream silk dupion
A piece of polyester wadding 10 x 20in (25 x 50cm)

Stitches: Long and short stitch, split backstitch,
stem stitch
Threads: Use one strand of crewel wool throughout

1 Prepare your fabric (see page 117); then trace the
flower outline on to it (see page 117); and mount it
into your hoop or frame (see page 117).
2 Read 'General Working Advice' (see page 117).
The picture on page 49 and the chart on page 52 will
help with placing the colours.
3 Begin with ecru and work a split backstitch outline
to the petals.
4 Still using ecru, work a row of long and short stitch
along the outer edge of each petal and then work
rows of light pink, mid pink and dark pink to the bottom of the petals. You may need to make two layers
of dark pink to fill the petals.
5 Outline the leaves in light green split backstitch
and then fill with long and short stitch (this will be
almost like satin stitch as the leaves are so narrow).
Add a few dark green stitches to the little leaf at the
base of the flower and to the underneath bit of the
right-hand leaf.
6 Work a row of dark green stem stitch along each
leaf centre. Work two or three rows of brown stem
stitch along the stems.
7 When complete, wash and press (see page 120) and
then make up (see page 123).

Magnolia cross stitch picture (left) and handerkerchief
purse (right).

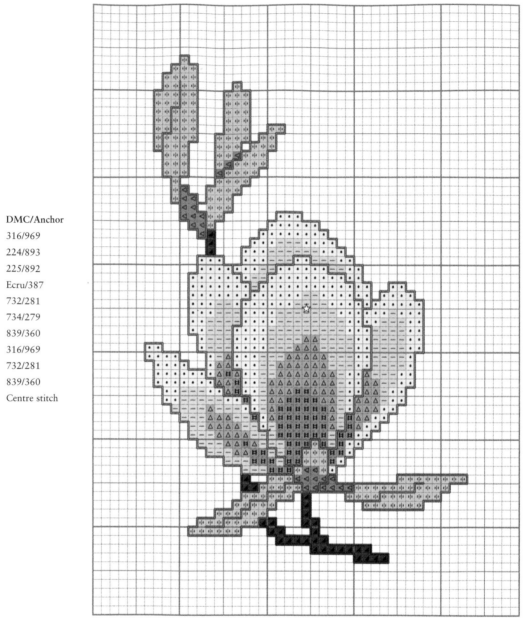

DMC/Anchor

⋈ ⋈	316/969
△ △	224/893
– –	225/892
• •	Ecru/387
◁ ◁	732/281
⋮ ⋮	734/279
◣ ◣	839/360
——	316/969
——	732/281
——	839/360
☆	Centre stitch

MAGNOLIA

	DMC	Anchor	Appleton
Dark pink	316	969	711
Mid pink	224	893	752
Light pink	225	892	881
Ecru	Ecru	387	882
Dark green	732	281	243
Light green	734	279	241
Brown	839	360	914
Optional outlines			
Flower	316	969	711
Leaves	732	281	243
Stems	839	360	914

In the Chinese flower calender,

magnolia is the flower of May and is

the symbol of feminine sweetness.

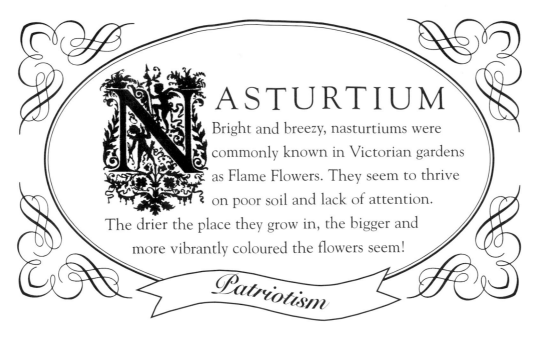

NASTURTIUM

Bright and breezy, nasturtiums were
commonly known in Victorian gardens
as Flame Flowers. They seem to thrive
on poor soil and lack of attention.
The drier the place they grow in, the bigger and
more vibrantly coloured the flowers seem!

Patriotism

Crewel Miniature

The second in a set of five miniatures. By choosing
only parts of the coloured drawing, I adapted the full
design to create an exquisite tiny project.

YOU WILL NEED

*8in (20cm) square, fine linen union
Appleton crewel wool (yarn) as listed in the
table on page 52
Size 7 crewel needle
An embroidery hoop*

Stitches: Long and short stitch, split backstitch,
French knots
Threads: Use one strand of crewel wool
(yarn) throughout

1 Prepare your fabric (see page 117); then trace the
flower outline on to it (see page 117) and mount it
into your hoop (see page 117).
2 Read 'General Working Advice' (see page 119).
The picture on this page and the chart on page 55
will help with placing the colours.
3 Begin with dark orange and work a split backstitch
outline to the whole flower, breaking off where the
petals are overlapped.
4 Still using dark orange, work a row of long and
short stitch along the outer edge then work rows in
light orange, then dark again, to the centre of the
flower. Take care at the centre of the flower to leave
gaps between the petals, and make the final stitches
seem to radiate out from a central point.
5 Using yellow and split backstitch, work a line about
half-way up each petal from the centre of the flower.
Allow these lines to curve slightly rather than being
completely straight.
6 Work up to five brown French knots in the centre.
7 Outline the leaves in pale green split backstitch,
and fill with long and short stitch in pale green.
Work the veins in dark green split backstitch.
8 When complete, wash and press (see page 120).
Mount and frame as required.

Nasturtium came from the West Indies

and was first called Indian cresses due

to its hot, peppery flavour.

Cross Stitch Pincushion

This pretty pincushion (pictured on page 69) will work equally well without the lace and satin piping.

Design size: 4¹/₂in (11cm) square
Stitch count: 57 x 51

YOU WILL NEED

8in (20cm) square, 28-count cream linen
Stranded cotton (floss) as listed on the chart on page 55
Size 26 tapestry needle
A 4¹/₂in (11.5cm) diameter wooden pincushion base
Satin piping and lace for trimming (optional)

Stitches: Cross stitch, backstitch, French knots
Threads: Use two strands of stranded cotton (floss) for the cross stitch and French knots, and one strand for the backstitch outline

1 Prepare your fabric (see page 112).
2 Following the chart on page 55 and starting at the centre, stitch the nasturtiums. Add three French knots in brown to the centre of each flower.
3 When complete, press (see page 113) and mount on the wooden base according to the manufacturer's instructions. If liked, add gathered lace and a satin piping, stapling them on to the edge of the pad before you set it into the wooden base.

Canvaswork Slippers

Small and dainty, these delightful slippers (pictured on page 57) definitely seem to be from a bygone, more ladylike age! The basic kit is available from specialist suppliers and although I worked different flowers on each one of mine, you will probably prefer to make yours as a matching pair.

YOU WILL NEED

A slipper-making kit (see Suppliers page 126)
Appleton crewel wool (yarn) as listed in the table on page 55 for the Nasturtium Slipper or page 61 for the Orange Blossom Slipper (a skein of each will make a pair)
One hank of Appleton crewel wool (yarn) 406 for the background
Appleton crewel wool (yarn) 475 for the lattice pattern (optional)
Size 22 tapestry needle.
A black waterproof felt tip pen
A sheet of tracing paper
Masking tape
An embroidery frame

Stitches: Tent stitch, diagonal tent stitch, long and short stitch, split backstitch, French knots
Threads: Use three strands of crewel wool (yarn) throughout unless otherwise stated in the text

The leaves and flowers of the nasturtium enhance a salad and the seeds can be pickled as a substitute for capers.

Nasturtium crewelwork miniature.

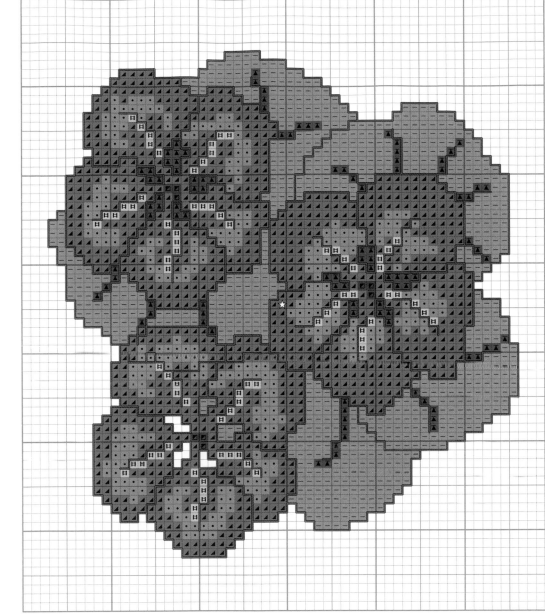

DMC/Anchor

◢◢	720/326
· ·	722/323
н н	725/306
▲▲	937/268
– –	470/266
◪◪	938/381
—	400/351
—	937/268
☆	Centre stitch

1 Choose which flowers you want to embroider, and trace their outlines on to the tracing paper. You can alter the shapes at this stage by moving the tracing around to achieve a different arrangement until you have a drawing that you are happy with.

2 Place the outline on a flat surface and secure it with masking tape. Lay the marked-out slipper shape on the canvas supplied in the kit centrally over the drawing and secure with masking tape. Make sure you have placed the drawing carefully.

3 Using the waterproof pen, draw all the lines that you can see quite clearly through the canvas.

4 Read 'General Working Advice' (see page 116). The pictures on pages 53 and 57, and the charts on pages 55 and 61, will help with placing the colours.

NASTURTIUM

	DMC	Anchor	Appleton
Dark orange	720	326	864
Light orange	722	323	862
Yellow	725	306	474
Dark green	937	268	254
Light green	470	266	253
Brown	938	381	956
Optional outlines			
Flowers	400	351	479
Leaves	937	268	254

THE NASTURTIUMS

1 Using dark orange, work a row of long and short stitch around the outer edge of the petals. Work the next layer in light orange, working from the centre of the flower outwards. Complete the petals using dark orange in the centre of the flower.

2 Work a row of split backstitch along the centre line of each petal just into the light orange, and then finish each flower with three brown French knots.

3 Work the leaves in light green long and short stitch, and add dark green veins in split backstitch.

THE ORANGE BLOSSOMS

1 Using white, work a row of long and short stitch around the outer edge of the petals. Work the next layer in very pale gold, working from the centre of the flower outwards. Complete the petals with a row of split backstitch along the centre line of each petal in very pale gold.

2 Add brown stamens in split backstitch using one strand, and add a gold French knot to the end of each, also in one strand.

3 Work the leaves in light green long and short stitch, and add dark green veins in split backstitch.

THE BACKGROUND

To add interest, you can stitch a simple square trellis through the background.

1 The top centre line of each slipper will be marked on the prepared canvas in your kit. Make the first gold tent stitch over the central thread at this point and work diagonal lines in both directions from it.

2 The trellis lines cross on every sixth stitch. Work them all to the edge of the slipper shape.

3 Fill in the dark green background using diagonal tent stitch.

4 Stretch (see page 116), then make up according to the kit instructions.

Nasturtium in common language

means 'nose-twister', a reference to its

peppery flavour.

*Orange blossom (left) and nasturtium (right)
canvaswork slippers.*

ORANGE BLOSSOM

The philadelphus or mock orange has held its popularity since Victorian times. Easy to grow, its white, heavily scented blossoms fill the early summer evenings.

Purity equals loveliness

Crewel Miniature

The third in a set of five miniatures featured in this book. As with the anemone and nasturtium miniatures I have only selected part of the coloured drawing – this time it was one flower, a bud and few leaves – moving them all around to create the perfect balance for this small picture.

YOU WILL NEED

8in (20cm) square, fine linen union
Appleton crewel wool (yarn) as listed in the
table on page 61
Size 7 crewel needle
An embroidery hoop

Stitches: Long and short stitch, split backstitch and French knots
Threads: Use one strand of crewel wool (yarn) throughout

1 Prepare your fabric (see page 117); then trace the flower outline on to it (see page 117) and mount it into your hoop.
2 Read 'General Working Advice' (see page 119). The picture on this page and the chart on page 61 will help with placing the colours.
3 Begin with white and work a split backstitch outline to the whole flower, breaking off where the petals are overlapped.
4 Still using white, work a row of long and short stitch along the outer edge of each petal, then work to the centre line of each petal with very pale gold.

Oranges and lemons,

Say the bells of St Clement's.

You owe me five farthings,

Say the bells of St Martin's.

Nursery rhyme

Orange blossom crewelwork miniature.

5 Using very pale gold and split backstitch, work a line about half-way up each petal from the centre of the flower. Allow these lines to curve slightly rather than being completely straight.

6 Work about nine gold French knots towards the centre of the flower. Make brown straight stitches joining each stamen to the centre of the flower. These should all seem to grow out of the same spot.

7 Outline all the petals of the bud in white. Using long and short stitch, fill the back ones in white, and the front one in white at the outer edge and very pale gold in the middle.

8 Outline the leaves in light green split backstitch, and fill with long and short stitch. Work the veins in dark green split backstitch.

9 Add the dark green stem to the bud in split backstitch, making a few stitches actually into the base of the bud.

10 When complete, wash and press (see page 120). Mount and frame as required.

O Love what hours were thine and mine,

In lands of palm and southern pine;

In lands of palm, of orange-blossom,

Of olive, aloe, and maize and vine.

Alfred, Lord Tennyson *The Daisy*

Cross Stitch Silk Cushion

Never choose fabric in haste; I was a little disappointed with this embroidery until I found the right silk which immediately brought it out of itself.

Design size: 4in (10cm) square
Stitch count: 57 x 51

YOU WILL NEED

10in (20cm) square, 28-count natural linen
Stranded cotton (floss) as listed on the chart on page 60
Size 26 tapestry needle
28in (70cm) silk dupion
Some cream silk dupion for piping

Stitches: Cross stitch, backstitch, French knots
Threads: Use two strands of stranded cotton (floss) for the cross stitch and French knots, and one strand for the backstitch outline

1 Prepare your fabric (see page 112).
2 Following the chart on page 61 and starting at the centre, stitch the orange blossoms. Add the stamens in a single strand of brown and make a gold French knot at the end of each one.
3 When complete, press (see page 113) and make up (see page 121).

Canvaswork Inset Velvet Pincushion

Such a tiny piece of embroidery using a scrap of 18-count canvas, an odd bit of velvet and left-over stranded cotton (floss) needs no detailed instructions. Choose a flower from the chart and work in tent stitch using six strands of stranded cotton (floss). Outline with two strands. Fill in a background in tent stitch using two strands of Appleton crewel wool (yarn), then add a border. Mount in gold velvet and add a twisted cord, knotted at each corner.

Delve into your collection of bits and pieces and try this with other flowers from this book. I guarantee you will make more than one!

Orange blossom cross stitch silk cushion.

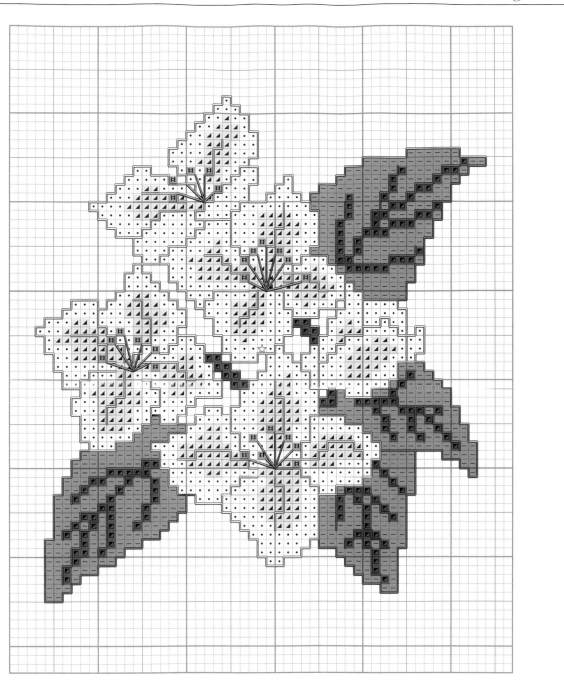

DMC/Anchor

• •	Blanc/1
◢ ◢	746/386
H H	783/307
	470/266
	937/268
——	783/307
——	937/268
——	938/381
☆	Centre stitch

Saracen brides in the times of the Crusades wore orange blossoms as a symbol of fecundity because the orange was such a prolific fruit-bearing tree. The blossoms were worn as an appeal to the spirit of the tree, that the bride should not be barren. They have been adopted ever since as bridal flowers throughout Europe and North America.

ORANGE BLOSSOM

	DMC	Anchor	Appleton
White	Blanc	1	992
Very pale gold	746	386	872
Gold	783	307	475
Light green	470	266	253
Dark green	937	268	254
Optional outlines			
Flower	783	307	475
Leaves	937	268	254
Stamen stalks	938	381	956

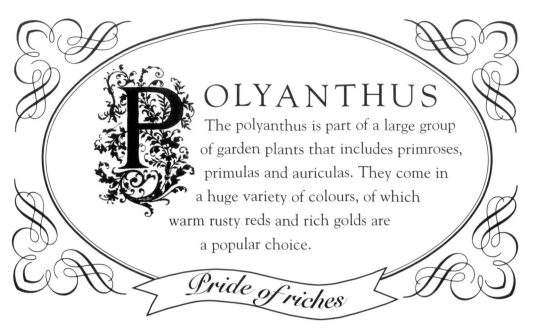

POLYANTHUS

The polyanthus is part of a large group
of garden plants that includes primroses,
primulas and auriculas. They come in
a huge variety of colours, of which
warm rusty reds and rich golds are
a popular choice.

Pride of riches

Crewelwork Picture

Compare this picture, pictured on page 91, with the
cross stitch version shown on page 66. Look at the
detailing of both of them carefully. Close to, you can
see how much more realistic an effect can be
achieved with this type of stitching.

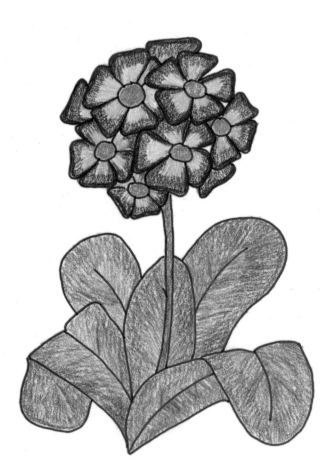

Compare this picture, pictured on page 91, with the cross stitch version shown on page 66.

YOU WILL NEED

10in (25cm) square, fine linen union
Appleton crewel wool (yarn) as listed in the table on
page 67
Size 7 crewel needle
An embroidery hoop or frame

Stitches: Long and short stitch, stem stitch, split
backstitch, French knots
Threads: Use one strand of crewel wool (yarn)
throughout

1 Prepare your fabric (see page 117); then trace the
flower outline on to it (see page 117) and mount it
into your hoop or frame.
2 Read 'General Working Advice' (see page 119).
The picture on this page and the chart on page 67
will help with placing the colours.
3 Work a row of mid green split backstitch around
the edge of the leaves.
4 Still using mid green, work a row of long and short
stitch along the outer edge of each leaf, then a row of
light green. Take care that the mid green row follows
the outer shape of the leaf and that all stitches radiate out from the centre.
5 Work the complete area of the leaf behind the stem
and then work the stem over your stitching as close
parallel lines of stem stitch in dark green.
6 Work the veins in dark green stem stitch.
7 Work each flower separately, completing one
before starting another. All stitches should radiate

Woodsmen from the New Forest treated

cuts with an ointment made from

primrose flowers boiled with lard.

Polyanthus crewelwork picture.

out from the centre of the flower. Begin at the outer edge of each flower in red long and short stitch. Bring the needle up on the outer edge and down towards the centre. Work light gold towards the centre of the flower, bringing the needle up at the centre and down through the red stitches, blending the colours.

8 Using dark mauve and split backstitch, outline each petal. Take these lines right to the individual centre of the flower and keep the stitches fairly small around the curves.

9 Fill the centre of each little flower with a tightly packed cluster of French knots.

10 When complete, wash and press (see page 120). Mount and frame as required.

In the Middle Ages a concoction made from primroses was used as a remedy for gout and rheumatism and an infusion of the roots was taken for nervous headaches. The flowers alone were also used to make love potions.

Woolwork Footstool

The embroidery on this delightful little inlaid footstool has been applied on to velvet in the manner of a medieval slip, a common technique used in the Middle Ages. Motifs would be worked on canvas by teams of professional embroiderers and then stitched on to fabrics to dress furnishings. It was a way of having embroidered bed hangings, for example, without working large areas of plain background.

YOU WILL NEED

10in (25cm) square, 14-count interlock canvas
Appleton crewel wool (yarn) as listed in the
table on page 67
Size 22 tapestry needle
An embroidery frame, if required
A piece of velvet measuring at least 4in (10cm) more
all round than the footstool you are using
A round footstool; the one pictured is 10in (25cm) in
diameter (see Suppliers page 126)

Stitches: Tent stitch, diagonal tent stitch, long legged cross stitch, long and short stitch, satin stitch, split backstitch, French knots
Threads: Use three strands of crewel wool (yarn) throughout

1 Enlarge the flower outline by 140% and trace on to your canvas (see page 115).
2 Mount the canvas into a frame if required (see page 114).
3 Read 'General Working Advice' (see page 116). The picture on page 62 and the chart on page 67 will help with placing the colours.
4 Using mid green, work a row of long and short stitch around the outer edges of the leaves.
5 Work the next row in light green, working from the centre of the leaves outwards.
6 Work the veins in dark green split stitch. Do not work the stem yet.
7 Work each flower separately, completing one before starting another. All the stitches should radiate out from the centre of the flower. Begin at the outer edge of each flower in red long and short stitch; come up on the outer edge and down towards the centre. Work light gold towards the centre of the flower; come up at the centre and down through the red stitches, blending the colours.
8 Using dark mauve and split backstitch, outline each petal. Take these lines to the centre of the flower, keeping all the stitches fairly small around the curves.
9 Fill the centre of each little flower with dark gold tent stitch and then cover this with a tightly packed cluster of French knots.

10 When flower and leaves are complete, stretch (see page 116).

11 Cut out the two pieces leaving ³⁄₈in (1cm) of unworked canvas around the embroidery. Turn in the unworked edges and tack the two pieces on to the velvet. Use the original drawing to help you place the two pieces.

12 Using mid green for the leaf section and dark mauve for the flowers, work two rows of split back-stitch around the pieces, following the shapes. Make sure that the inner row is worked through the canvas edge to attach the embroidery. Work the second row against the canvas edge, covering any white canvas edges that may be showing. Make your split back-stitch quite large and pull the stitches quite tightly.

13 Now add the stem as three rows of split backstitch in dark green. Begin at the bottom and work over the leaf and on across the velvet to join the leaves to the flower. If necessary refer to the drawing to help you place the line.

14 Mount the applied embroidery on to the footstool following the manufacturer's instructions. If liked, staple silk piping into the sides of the pad before you set it into the wooden base.

Cross Stitch Picture

The mellow tones of the burr walnut frame work beautifully with the colours of the picture, giving an antique feel to the finished piece.

Design size: 4 x 3in (10 x 8cm)
Stitch count: 61 x 42

YOU WILL NEED

10 x 8in (25 x 20cm) 28-count cream linen
Stranded cotton (floss) as listed on the chart on page 67
Size 26 tapestry needle

Stitches: Cross stitch, backstitch
Threads: Use two strands of stranded cotton (floss) for the cross stitch and one strand for the backstitch outline

1 Prepare your fabric (see page 112).
2 Following the chart on page 67 and starting at the centre, stitch the polyanthus.
3 Use the alphabet of your choice (see page 106) to add the name.
4 When complete, press (see page 113). Mount and frame as required.

Polyanthus cross stitch picture.

DMC/Anchor	
■	3777/20
H H	782/308
· ·	742/303
▨	936/846
▲◢	732/281
– –	733/280
▬	902/72
▬	936/846
▬	732/281
☆	Centre stitch

POLYANTHUS

	DMC	Anchor	Appleton
Red	3777	20	725
Dark gold	782	308	475
Light gold	742	303	473
Dark green	936	846	336
Mid green	732	281	334
Light green	733	280	333
Optional outlines			
Flowers	902	72	715
Leaves	936	846	336
Stem	732	281	334

In Glamorganshire, graves would often be bedecked with flowers. No evergreens or flowers are permitted to be planted on graves, but such as are sweet scented: the pink and polyanthus, sweet Williams, gilliflowers, and carnations, mignonette, thyme, hyssop, chamomile, and rosemary make up the usual decorations.

Rev H Friend *Flowers and Folklore Vol 1*

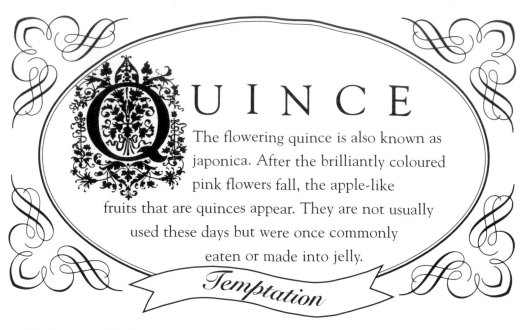

QUINCE

The flowering quince is also known as japonica. After the brilliantly coloured pink flowers fall, the apple-like fruits that are quinces appear. They are not usually used these days but were once commonly eaten or made into jelly.

Temptation

Herb Pillow

I filled my herb pillow with ordinary pot pourri. Fill yours with herbs that induce peaceful sleep, and you have the perfect bedroom pillow.

Design size: 4¹/₂ x 3¹/₂in (11 x 9cm)
Stitch count: 64 x 52

YOU WILL NEED

8in (20cm) square, 28-count cream linen
Stranded cotton (floss) as listed on the chart on page 70
Size 26 tapestry needle
10in (25cm) printed cotton fabric
1²/₃yd (1.5m) wide lace
Calico for lining
Pot pourri or sleeping herbs
Polyester filling

Stitches: Cross stitch, backstitch, French knots
Threads: Use two strands of stranded cotton (floss) for the cross stitch and French knots, and one strand for the straight stitches and backstitch outline

1 Prepare your fabric (see page 112).
2 Following the chart on page 70 and starting at the centre, stitch the quince blossoms.
3 Work the stalks of the stamens in brown straight stitches and add a yellow French knot to the end of each one.
4 When complete, press (see page 113) and make up (see page 121). This is only a small pillow, measuring about 9in (23cm) square. If you prefer a larger one, make up according to the instructions for an inset cushion with mitred corners, adding a gathered lace frill and a bow to trim.

A bowl of ripe quinces will

sweetly scent a room.

Opposite: *Quince herb pillow (top) and nasturtium pincushion (bottom).*

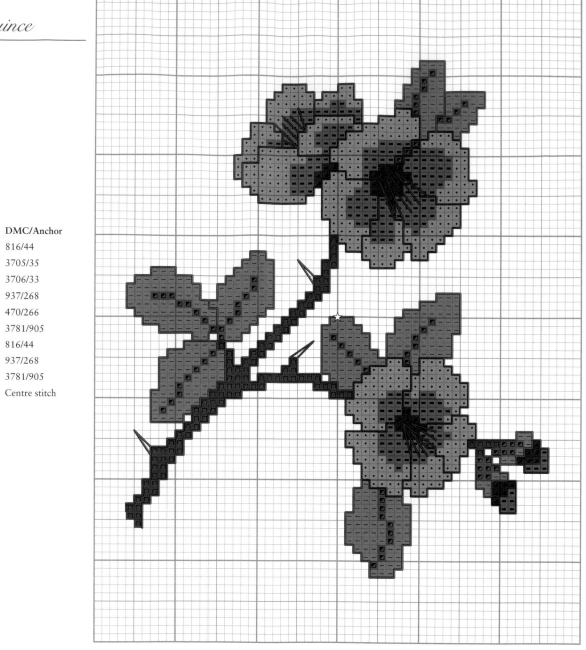

DMC/Anchor

816/44	
3705/35	
3706/33	
937/268	
470/266	
3781/905	
——	816/44
——	937/268
——	3781/905
☆	Centre stitch

QUINCE

	DMC	Anchor	Appleton
Dark pink	816	44	948
Mid pink	3705	35	945
Light pink	3706	33	943
Dark green	937	268	256
Light green	470	266	254
Brown	3781	905	916
French knots	742	303	474
Optional outlines			
Flowers	816	44	948
Leaves	937	268	256
Stems and			
stamen stalks	3781	905	916

They dined on mince and slices of quince,

Which they ate with a runcible spoon;

And hand in hand, on the edge of the sand,

They danced by the light of the moon.

Edward Lear *The Owl and the Pussycat*

70

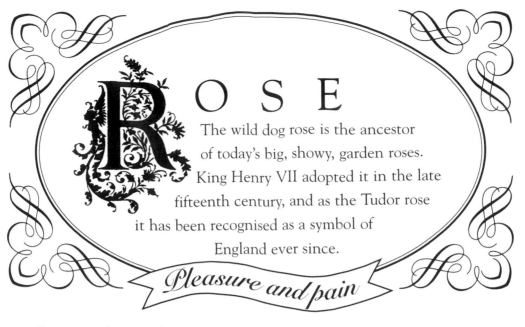

ROSE

The wild dog rose is the ancestor of today's big, showy, garden roses. King Henry VII adopted it in the late fifteenth century, and as the Tudor rose it has been recognised as a symbol of England ever since.

Pleasure and pain

Crewelwork Frilled Silk Cushion

This beautiful silk cushion is really a decorative object. For a more everyday version, stitch it in canvaswork from the chart and finish it in linen union.

YOU WILL NEED

12in (30cm) square, fine cream linen union
Appleton crewel wool (yarn) as listed in the table on page 72
Size 7 crewel needle
An embroidery hoop or small frame
31½in (80cm) cream silk dupion for making up

Stitches: Split backstitch, long and short stitch, French knots, stem stitch
Threads: Use one strand of crewel wool (yarn) throughout

1 Prepare your fabric (see page 117); then trace the flower outline on to it (see page 117) and mount it into your hoop or frame (see page 117).
2 Read 'General Working Advice' (see page 119). The picture on this page and the chart on page 72 will help with placing the colours.
3 Begin with palest pink and work a split backstitch outline to the three petals on the right-hand side of the large flower.
4 Still using palest pink, work a row of long and short stitch along the outer edge of each petal and then work rows of light pink, mid pink and dark pink to the middle of the flower.
5 Outline the turned-over edges of the two left-hand petals in split backstitch in dark pink. Work long and short stitch over this in dark and mid pink to fill. Complete the petals in the same way as the first three.
6 Add randomly placed French knots in gold close to the centre of the rose and a cluster of gold French knots in the middle.
7 Outline the leaves in mid green split backstitch and fill with long and short stitch from the edge to the centre vein. Add tiny stitches to make the spiky edges. Work the veins in light green split backstitch.
8 Work the petals of the larger bud in long and short stitch underlined with split backstitch, shading from

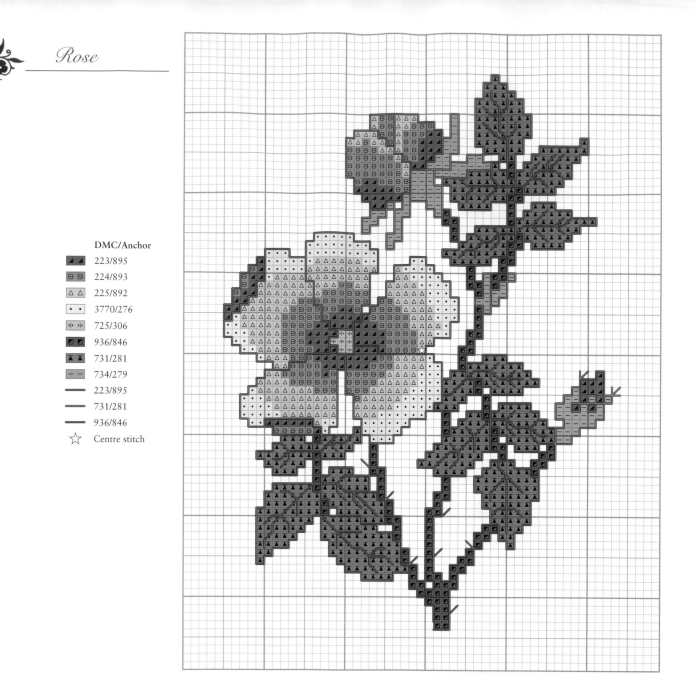

DMC/Anchor

▲▲	223/895
B B	224/893
△ △	225/892
· ·	3770/276
·ı· ·ı·	725/306
▞ ▞	936/846
▲ ▲	731/281
– –	734/279
——	223/895
——	731/281
——	936/846
☆	Centre stitch

ROSE

	DMC	Anchor	Appleton
Dark pink	223	895	223
Mid pink	224	893	222
Light pink	225	892	221
Palest pink	3770	276	202
Gold	725	306	472
Dark green	936	846	336
Mid green	731	281	334
Light green	734	279	333
French knots	725	306	472
Optional outlines			
Flower	223	895	223
Bud leaves	731	281	334
Leaves and stems	936	846	336

palest pink at the outer edge to dark pink at the base.
9 Work the bud leaves in long and short stitch in light green – with no split backstitch underline – from the tip of each leaf to the base of the flower. Work the pale leaves at the base of the upper leaves and the lower bud in the same way.
10 Finally, work the stems in dark green stem stitch with added small stitches to make the thorns.
11 When complete, wash, press (see page 120) and make up (see page 121).

Opposite: Clockwise from top left: Rose crewel miniature, crewelwork frilled silk cushion, cross stitch hand mirror and velvet-backed canvaswork pincushion.

Cross Stitch Hand Mirror

To make the design small enough to fit the circle I stitched on 36-count linen. You could use 28-count and make the design smaller by missing out the bud and leaf spray at the top.

Design size: 4 x 2³/₄in (10 x 7cm) on 36-count
5 x 3¹/₂in (13 x 9cm) on 28-count
Stitch count: 69 x 49

YOU WILL NEED

7in (18cm) square, 36-count natural linen
Stranded cottons (floss) as listed on the chart on page 72
Size 26 tapestry needle
A wooden hand mirror (see Suppliers, page 126)

Stitches: Cross stitch, backstitch, French knots
Threads: Use one strand of stranded cotton (floss) for the cross stitch, the backstitch outline and the French knots

1 Prepare your fabric (see page 112).
2 Following the chart on page 72 and starting at the centre, stitch the rose. Scatter French knots in gold on the centre of the flower and on the petals near the centre – give some a straight stitch as a stalk.
3 Use the alphabet of your choice (see page 106) to add the name.
4 When complete, press (see page 113) and attach according to the manufacturer's instructions. I also added silk piping around the edge.

The Christian martyr, Saint Dorothy, was put to death in about AD 300. It is said that at her trial a lawyer asked her to send him flowers from the garden of heaven. On the day of Dorothy's execution he received roses, delivered by a messenger, even though it was the depths of winter.

A CURE FOR INSOMNIA AND MELANCHOLY

In a little bag, put the dried petals and leaves of roses, also some powdered mint and cloves. Placed by the bed this scent should induce sleep and at other times cheer the soul.

Crewel Miniature

The fourth in a set of five miniatures. I like to mount small pieces of embroidery like this in quite heavy deep frames so that you have the impression of looking into something to see the embroidery.

YOU WILL NEED

8in (20cm) square, fine linen union
Appleton crewel wool (yarn) as listed in the table on page 72
Size 7 crewel needle
An embroidery hoop or small frame

Stitches: Split backstitch, long and short stitch and French knots
Threads: Use one strand of crewel wool (yarn) throughout

1 Follow steps 1 to 7 of the Rose Crewelwork Frilled Silk Cushion (see page 71).
2 When complete, wash and press (see page 120). Mount and frame as required.

Velvet-backed Canvaswork Pincushion

This little pincushion shows what can be done with a small scrap of canvas, a little bit of velvet and some left-over wool (yarn). Working from the chart, stitch the bud and its leaf in tent stitch. Surround closely with a border of tent stitch and long legged cross stitch, then fill in the background in tent stitch. Back with velvet. Pad the little cushion with some polyester filling and stitch up. You have a gift for someone to treasure and it will have taken no more than an evening to complete!

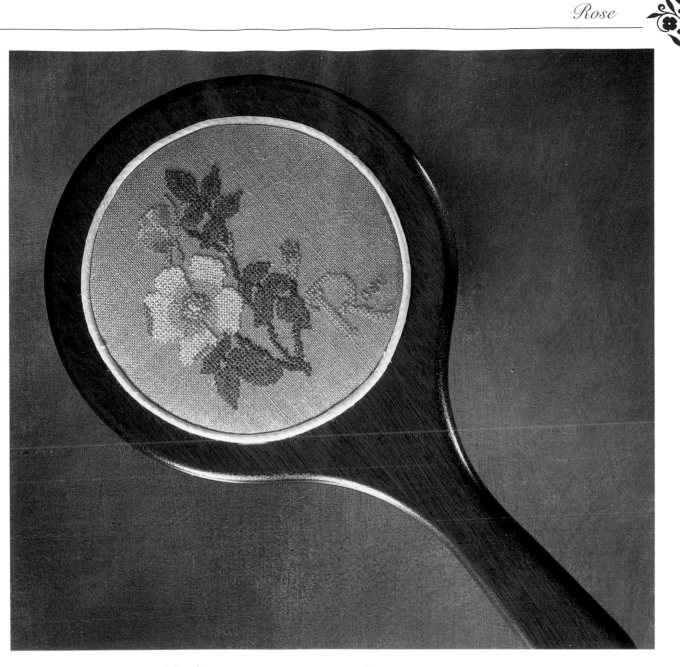

Rose cross stitch hand mirror.

RECIPE FOR ROSEHIP TEA

One teaspoon dried rosehips

One cup boiling water

Sugar or honey to taste

Pour boiling water over the rosehips,
cover and leave to stand for five minutes.
Strain and add the sugar or honey.

RECIPE FOR ROSE PETAL JAM

1½lb (675g) rose petals

12oz (300g) sugar

12oz (300g) honey

Three tablespoons lemon juice

Simmer the petals in a small amount of
water until tender. Add the sugar, honey and
lemon juice and cook gently until the
mixture is thick and syrupy. Allow to cool
and pour into warm, sterilized jars and seal.

SUNFLOWER

Big, yellow sunflowers are said to always keep their faces turned to the sun and follow it in its daily path across the sky. This may be poetic licence but it is a pleasing idea and there can be no doubt as to how the sunflower got its name.

Haughtiness

Woolwork Beaded Pillow

The centre of a sunflower with its almost geometrically placed seeds immediately suggested beadwork on canvas to me. The result was this delightful velvet pillow which, while not practical for everyday use, makes a wonderfully decorative cushion.

YOU WILL NEED

12in (30cm) square, 14-count double thread (Penelope) canvas
Mill Hill seed beads as listed in the table on page 77
Appleton crewel wool (yarn) as listed in the table on page 77
1 hank Appleton crewel wool 725 for the background
Neutral coloured polyester sewing thread
Size 22 tapestry needle
A beading needle
A black waterproof felt tip pen
A sheet of tracing paper
Masking tape
An embroidery frame

Stitches: Diagonal tent stitch, long legged cross stitch, long and short stitch, split backstitch, French knots, half cross stitch
Threads: Use three strands of crewel wool (yarn) throughout unless otherwise stated in the text

1 Enlarge the flower outline by 140% and trace on to your canvas (see page 115).
2 Mount the canvas into your frame if required.

Ah, Sun-flower! Weary of time,

Who countest the steps of the Sun;

Seeking after that sweet golden clime,

Where the traveller's journey is done.

William Blake Ah, *Sun-Flower*

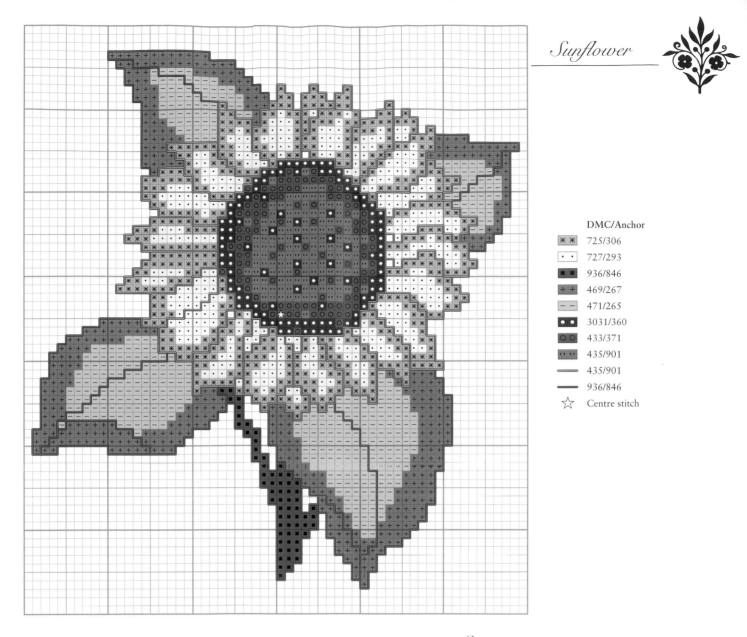

	DMC/Anchor
✳ ✳	725/306
· ·	727/293
■ ·	936/846
+ +	469/267
– –	471/265
◨ ·	3031/360
◎ ◎	433/371
▦ ▦	435/901
—	435/901
—	936/846
☆	Centre stitch

3 Read 'General Working Advice' (see page 116). The picture on page 76 and the chart on this page will help with placing the colours.

4 Begin stitching the petals. Using mid yellow work a row of long and short stitch around the outer edge of the petals.

5 Work the next layer in pale yellow, working from the centre of the flower outwards. Outline all the petals in dark yellow split backstitch using one strand.

6 Fill the centre of the flower with mixed beads. Tip a few of each colour into a small dish and pick them at random. Thread the beading needle with sewing thread and work in half cross stitch attaching a bead with each stitch (see page 120). Work back and forth across the rows until the entire centre is filled. Work a row of dark yellow French knots to surround the beadwork and fill any gaps between the beads and the petals.

7 Work the leaves in both mid green and light green using long and short stitch, adding dark green split backstitch veins.

SUNFLOWER

	DMC	Anchor	Appleton
Dark yellow	782	308	475
Mid yellow	725	306	474
Pale yellow	727	293	471
Dark green	936	846	256
Mid green	469	267	254
Light green	471	265	253
Dark brown	3031	360	582
Mid brown	433	371	767
Light brown	435	901	765
Rust			725
Optional outlines			
Flower	435	901	765
Leaves and stem	936	846	256

Mill Hill seed beads

Copper	00330
Gold	02011

8 Work the stems in long and short stitch, beginning at the top of each stem, working down to the bottom.

9 To mark the beaded border lines, count two double threads to the left of the lower left leaf and eight double threads to the right of the upper right leaf. Draw in pencil lines and then count out another six threads and draw another line on each side. These lines mark the six-bead border twist.

10 Count a further four threads and draw another line. This marks the extent of the background. To mark the background lines top and bottom, count 14 threads from the end of the stem and 18 from the top leaf. Turn to page 110 for the chart. I did not use the outer border lines on the chart, only the twist and have used only the sides and not the top and bottom or any corners. Begin at the top counting from the chart attaching a bead for each symbol, alternating the bead colours for each twist. Repeat the design until you reach the outer pencil lines at the bottom.

11 Fill in the background in rust using diagonal tent stitch working it carefully around the beaded borders. Finally work a row of long legged cross stitch to complete and frame the panel.

12 Stretch (see page 116), make tassels and cords (see page 125) and make up (see page 121).

Cross Stitch Cushion

Compare this bright cushion with the velvet beaded pillow on page 76. The same design takes on a totally different character in different threads, stitches and fabrics.

Design size: 4¹⁄₂ x 4in (11.5 x 10cm)
Stitch count: 64 x 58

YOU WILL NEED

12in (30cm) square, 28-count natural linen
Stranded cotton (floss) as listed on the chart on page 77
Size 26 tapestry needle
20in (50cm) furnishing fabric

Stitches: Cross stitch, backstitch
Threads: Use two strands of stranded cotton (floss) for the cross stitch and one strand for the backstitch outline

1 Prepare your fabric (see page 112).
2 Following the chart on page 77 and starting at the centre, stitch the sunflower.
3 When complete, press (see page 113) and make up (see page 121).

Tulip (left) and sunflower (right) cross stitch panel cushions.

TULIP

From tiny miniatures to great big showy blooms, tulips have always been extremely popular. In Holland, where rival bulb growers raced to produce exotic varieties and colours, bulbs changed hands for enormous prices.

Fame

Woolwork Pillow

With its rich colours this pillow (pictured on page 83) would look stunning when grouped with the anemone pillow (page 10). You will notice in the picture on page 83 that I used three greens in the leaves of this tulip, but only two are shown on the chart. I used the lightest green on the leaves rather than outlining in backstitch. When you stitch the green, use the photograph of the tulip to guide you.

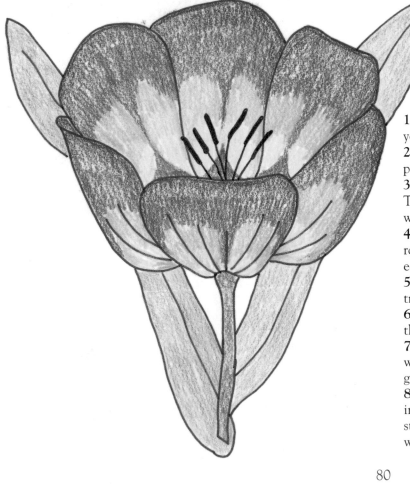

YOU WILL NEED

12in (30cm) square, 14-count interlock canvas
Appleton crewel wool (yarn) as listed in the table on page 81
(3 skeins each are required of 725, 475 and 244 and 1 hank of 692) for the background
Size 22 tapestry needle
An embroidery frame
20in (50cm) velvet for making up

Stitches: Tent stitch, diagonal tent stitch, long legged cross stitch, long and short stitch, satin stitch, split backstitch, bullion knots
Threads: Use three strands of crewel wool (yarn) throughout unless otherwise stated in the text

1 Enlarge the flower outline by 140% and trace on to your canvas (see page 115).

2 Mount the canvas into your frame if required (see page 114).

3 Read 'General Working Advice' (see page 116). The picture on this page and the chart on page 81 will help with placing the colours.

4 Begin stitching the flower. Using dark red, work a row of long and short stitch along the top to form the edge of the petals.

5 Work the next layer in red, working from the centre of the flower outwards.

6 Complete the petals using dark gold, light gold and then brown in the centre of the flower.

7 Outline the petals with red split backstitch and work in a few stitches on the petals in light gold to give a little colour variation.

8 Work eight to nine randomly placed bullion knots in the centre of the flower in brown to form the stamens and join them to the centre of the flower with straight stitches in pale green.

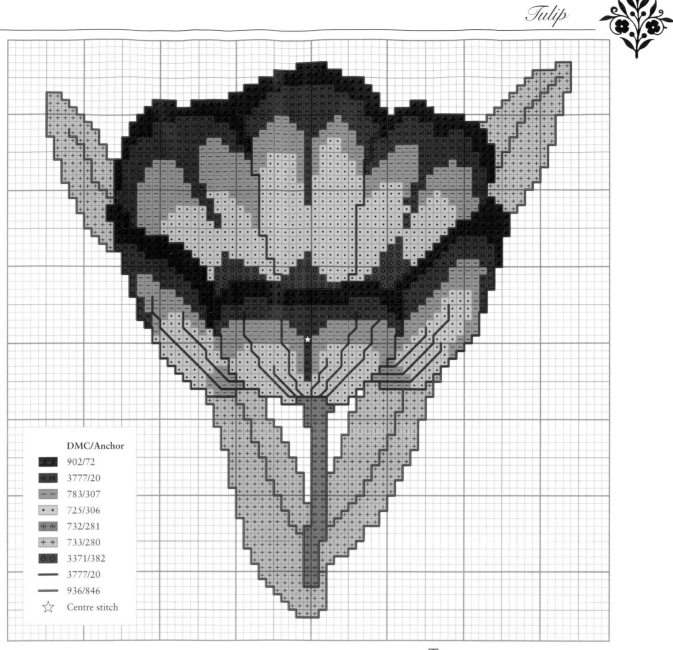

	DMC/Anchor
■■	902/72
K K	3777/20
– –	783/307
•·•	725/306
◈·◈	732/281
+ +	733/280
O O	3371/382
——	3777/20
——	936/846
☆	Centre stitch

Here tulips bloom as they are told;

Unkempt about these hedges blows

An English unofficial rose.

Rupert Brooke

TULIP

	DMC	Anchor	Appleton
Dark red	902	72	128
Red	3777	20	725
Dark gold	783	307	475
Light gold	725	306	474
Pale gold			692
Dark green	732	281	244
Light green	733	280	242
Pale green			331
Brown	3371	382	586
Bullion knots	3371	382	586
Optional outlines			
Flower	3777	20	725
Leaves and stem	936	846	245

An oriental legend tells that a Persian youth, Ferhad, became enamoured with the maiden, Shirin, who rejected his love. Ferhad went out into the desert to die of a broken heart. As he wept for his lost love and pined away, every tear falling into the barren sand turned into a beautiful blossom. These tulips became a symbol of the perfect lover.

9 Work the leaves in long and short stitch using the two lighter greens, and then work the central vein in dark green.

10 Work the length of the stem in light green long and short stitch.

11 To include the flower name, use the alphabet of your choice (see page 106). Work the large T in tent stitch and the rest of the work in backstitch letters once the background is complete.

12 Count a square that is 97 x 97 canvas threads to surround the design. Use pins to mark the square as you count so you can adjust to surround the flower. Allow the flower to cross this line in places where you need to – see the picture on the right. When you have decided on the correct placement, draw a pencil line in the canvas groove that surrounds these 97 threads in each direction.

13 Work the background in pale gold diagonal tent stitch taking care to tuck the stitches under the long and short stitch of the design. Complete the word in backstitch if you are using it. Work a single row of light green tent stitch on the thread outside the background. This green line is the inner line of the border.

14 Turn to page 110 for the twisted border pattern, and work in tent stitch from the chart in dark gold and red. Omit the outer line of the border and substitute a row of light green long legged cross stitch (see page 115) to complete and frame the panel.

15 When complete, stretch (see page 116), make the tassels and cords (see page 125) and make up (see page 121).

Sunflower woolwork beaded pillow (left) and tulip woolwork cushion (right).

Cross Stitch Cushion

This cushion, along with the sunflower one on page 78, would take pride of place in a sunny conservatory.

Design size: 5in (13cm) square
Stitch count: 73 x 69

YOU WILL NEED

12in (30cm) square, 28-count natural linen
Stranded cotton (floss) as listed on the chart on page 81
Size 26 tapestry needle
20in (50cm) furnishing fabric

Stitches: Cross stitch, backstitch, straight stitch, bullion knots
Threads: Use two strands of stranded cotton (floss) for the cross stitch and bullion knots, and one strand for the straight stitches and backstitch outline

1 Prepare your fabric (see page 112).
2 Following the chart on page 81 and starting at the centre, stitch the tulip.

3 Work eight to nine randomly placed bullion knots in the centre of the flower and join them to the centre with straight stitches in pale green.
4 When complete, press (see page 113) and make up (see page 121).

The tulip and the butterfly

Appear in brighter coats than I:

Let me be dress'd as fine as I will,

Flies, worms, and flowers, exceed me still.

Dr Isaac Watts *Against Pride in Clothes*

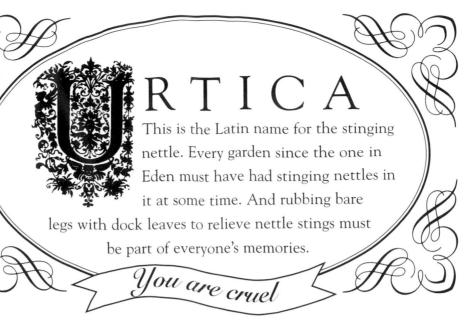

URTICA

This is the Latin name for the stinging nettle. Every garden since the one in Eden must have had stinging nettles in it at some time. And rubbing bare legs with dock leaves to relieve nettle stings must be part of everyone's memories.

You are cruel

Cross Stitch Picture

Mounted in dark green silk, the nettle cross stitch picture looks like an old botanical painting.

Design size: 6 x 3¹/₂in (15 x 9cm)
Stitch count: 87 x 48

YOU WILL NEED

12 x 10in (30 x 25cm) 28-count natural linen
Stranded cotton (floss) as listed on the chart on page 86
Size 26 tapestry needle
Dark green silk dupion for covering mount (optional)
Polyester wadding for padding

Stitches: Cross stitch, backstitch, French knots
Threads: Use two strands of stranded cotton (floss) for the cross stitch and French knots, and one strand for the backstitch outline

1 Prepare your fabric (see page 112).
2 Following the chart on page 86 and starting at the centre, stitch the nettle. Add some clusters of French knots in ecru where the stems of the top sets of leaves join the main stem.
3 Use the alphabet of your choice (see page 106) to add the name.
4 When complete, press (see page 113). Make a covered mount (see page 121) and frame as required.

Nettle leaves are still eaten as a vegetable by some country people. When boiled they taste similar to spinach.

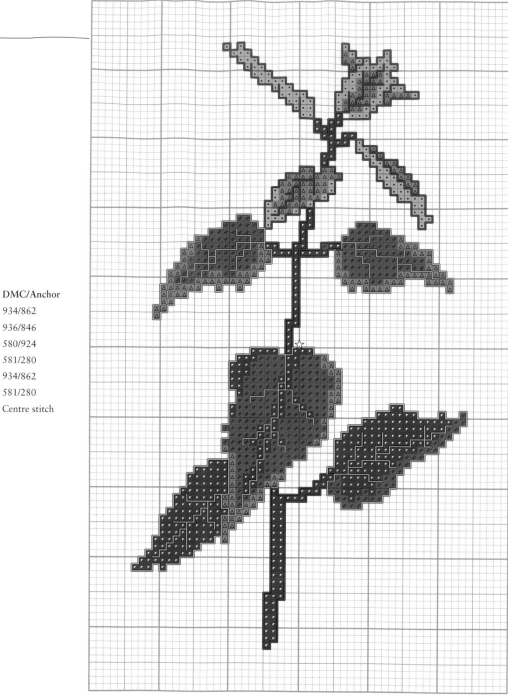

DMC/Anchor

▰ ▰	934/862
▨ ▨	936/846
△ △	580/924
• •	581/280
——	934/862
——	581/280
☆	Centre stitch

URTICA

	DMC	Anchor	Appleton
Dark green	934	862	407
Mid green	936	846	256
Light green	580	924	254
Lightest green	581	280	253
French knots	Ecru	387	882
Optional outlines			
Top leaves	934	862	407
Five lower leaves	581	280	253
Stems	934	862	407

Tender-handed stroke a nettle,

And it stings you for your pains;

Grasp it like a man of mettle,

And it soft as silk remains.

Aaron Hill

Opposite: *Urtica (top) and yarrow (bottom) pictures.*

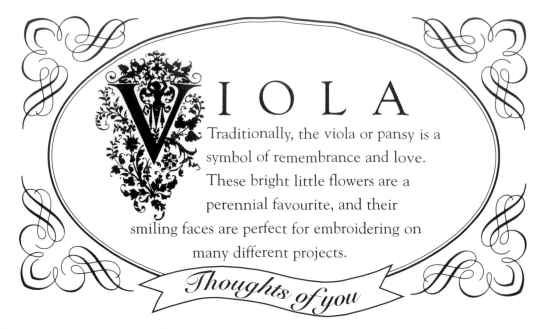

VIOLA

Traditionally, the viola or pansy is a symbol of remembrance and love. These bright little flowers are a perennial favourite, and their smiling faces are perfect for embroidering on many different projects.

Thoughts of you

Cross Stitch Picture

Pansies come in a huge variety of different colour combinations, so you can stitch these projects in a number of different colourways.

Design size: 4 x 3¹/₂in (10 x 9cm)
Stitch count: 57 x 51

YOU WILL NEED

10in (25cm) square, 28-count cream linen
Stranded cotton (floss) as listed on the chart on page 92
Size 26 tapestry needle

Stitches: Cross stitch, backstitch
Threads: Use two strands of stranded cotton (floss) for the cross stitch and one strand for the backstitch outline

1 Prepare your fabric (see page 112).
2 Following the chart on page 92 and starting at the centre, stitch the viola.
3 When complete, press (see page 113). Mount and frame as required.

Crewel Miniature

The fifth in a set of five miniatures. I traced one flower and four leaf tips but, because my drawing was smaller than the other four in the set, this time I enlarged it by 140% on a photocopier.

YOU WILL NEED

8in (20cm) square, fine linen union
Appleton crewel wool (yarn) as listed in the table on page 92
Size 7 crewel needle
An embroidery hoop

Stitches: Long and short stitch, split backstitch, French knots
Threads: Use one strand of crewel wool (yarn) throughout

1 Choose one of the violas to trace, and follow steps 1 and 2 of the Viola Crewelwork Picture on page 89, remembering to enlarge your drawing by 140%.
2 Follow the remaining steps for the Viola Crewelwork Picture, only working one flowerhead.

Crewelwork Picture

The viola, geranium and polyanthus set of pictures, all pictured on page 91, are excellent projects for improving your crewelwork skills.

YOU WILL NEED

10in (25cm) square, fine linen union
Appleton crewel wool (yarn) as listed in the
table on page 92
Size 7 crewel needle
An embroidery hoop or frame

Stitches: Long and short stitch, stem stitch, split backstitch, French knots
Threads: Use one strand of crewel wool (yarn) throughout

1 Prepare your fabric (see page 117); then trace the flower outline on to it (see page 117) and mount it into your hoop or frame.
2 Read 'General Working Advice' (see page 119). The picture on page 88 and the chart on page 92 will help with placing the colours.

This smiling-faced flower probably

has more names than any other – pansy,

love-in-idleness, 'kiss-me-quick'

and heartsease.

Cross stitch picture.

3 Work a row of dark green split backstitch around the edge of the leaves.

4 Still using dark green, work a row of long and short stitch along the outer edge of each leaf, then a row of light green.

5 Work the veins in dark green stem stitch.

6 Work each flower separately, completing one before starting another. All the stitches should radiate out from the centre of the flower. Outline each petal in split backstitch: the top two in dark mauve and the bottom three in dark gold.

7 Fill the petals with long and short stitch. Work the top two in mauve: with dark mauve, come up on the outer edge, over the split backstitch, and down towards the centre; with light mauve, come up at the centre and down through the dark mauve stitches, blending the colours.

8 Work the lower three petals in the same way, in dark gold at the outer edge shading through light gold, a few stitches of light mauve and finishing with brown at the centre of the flower.

9 Fill the centre of each flower with a tightly packed cluster of about seven to nine French knots.

10 When complete, wash and stretch (see page 120). Mount and frame as required.

Ran for sweethearts mad and died.

Love, in pity of their tears

And their loss in blooming years,

For their restless here-spent hours,

Gave them Heart's-ease turned to flowers.

Robert Herrick

From left to right: *Geranium,* viola *and* polyanthus crewelwork pictures.

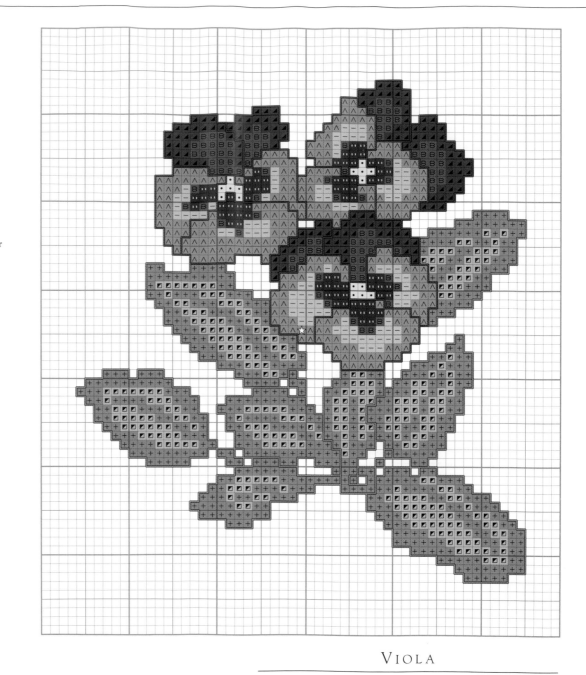

DMC/Anchor

◣◢	315/896
B B	316/969
∧ ∧	783/307
– –	676/891
+ +	732/281
◪ ◪	733/280
∷ ∷	3371/382
• •	Ecru/ 387
——	315/896
——	732/281
☆	Centre stitch

The juice of love-in-idleness

. . . on sleeping eyelids laid,

Will make man or woman madly dote

Upon the first live creature that it sees.

Shakespeare *A Midsummer Night's Dream*

VIOLA

	DMC	Anchor	Appleton
Dark mauve	315	896	715
Light mauve	316	969	714
Dark gold	783	307	473
Light gold	676	891	472
Dark green	732	281	334
Light green	733	280	333
Pale green			331
Brown	3371	382	588
Ecru	Ecru	387	872
Optional outlines			
Flowers	315	896	715
Leaves and stems	732	281	334

Woolwork Wooden-based Pincushion

I just took the flowers, then added three leaves to fit the pincushion circle. Rather than enlarge the design to suit the canvas, as on other projects, I used a fine 18-count canvas.

YOU WILL NEED

8in (20cm) square, 18-count interlock canvas
Appleton crewel wool (yarn) as listed in the table on page 92
2 skeins Appleton 331 for the background
Size 22 tapestry needle
An embroidery frame
A 4¹⁄₂in (11.5cm) diameter wooden pincushion base (see Suppliers on page 126)

Stitches: Long and short stitch, split backstitch, French knots, tent stitch
Threads: Use two strands of crewel wool (yarn) throughout

1 Prepare your fabric (see page 117), then trace the flower outline on to it (see page 117) and mount it into your frame (see page 117).
2 Read 'General Working Advice' (see page 119). The picture on page 88 and the chart on page 92 will help with placing the colours.
3 Begin by stitching the flowers. Using dark gold, work a row of long and short stitch around the outer edge of the lower petals.
4 Work the next layer in light gold, working from the centre of the flower outwards.
5 To complete the design, follow the instructions for the Crewelwork Picture on page 89 up to and including step 9, omitting any split backstitch underlines which apply only to crewelwork and are not suitable for use on canvas.
6 When complete, draw a circle 4¹⁄₂in (11.5cm) in diameter to surround it. Fill this circle with diagonal tent stitch in pale green. Where the tent stitch comes up against the embroidery, tuck it in well so that no canvas threads are allowed to show.
7 Stretch (see page 120) and mount on the pincushion base according to the manufacturer's instructions.

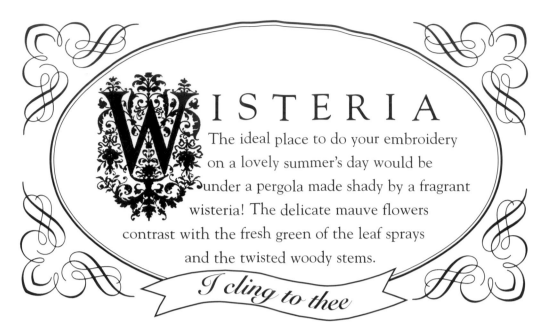

WISTERIA

The ideal place to do your embroidery on a lovely summer's day would be under a pergola made shady by a fragrant wisteria! The delicate mauve flowers contrast with the fresh green of the leaf sprays and the twisted woody stems.

I cling to thee

Cross Stitch Layette Basket

Take care to choose a fine fabric that will gather easily to make all the frills; the Liberty lawn shown on page 97 is ideal.

Design size: 4¹/₂ x 3¹/₂in (11 x 9cm)
Stitch count: 61 x 50

YOU WILL NEED

10 x 8in (25 x 20cm) 28-count cream evenweave
Stranded cotton (floss) as listed on the chart on page 95
Size 26 tapestry needle
Printed cotton fabric for making up
Polyester wadding
Wicker basket

Stitches: Cross stitch, backstitch
Threads: Use two strands of stranded cotton (floss) for the cross stitch and one strand for the backstitch outline
Basket: You can use whatever shape or size basket you like, although it would be sensible to choose a simple shape. Straight-sided baskets are ideal – curved shapes are more difficult to fit with a liner

1 Prepare your fabric (see page 112).
2 Following the chart on page 95 and starting at the centre, stitch the wisteria.
3 When complete, press (see page 113).
4 Make the padded liner and lid to fit your basket. Quantities for the fabric and specific instructions will depend entirely on the basket that you use. As a general guide, make a paper pattern first, cutting the pieces larger rather than smaller as you can always trim them later.
5 Once you are happy with the shape and size of the pattern make the liner. Cut out two pieces each in the fabric and one of polyester wadding. Lay the wadding between the two layers of fabric and quilt either by hand or sewing machine. Sew the pieces together to fit your basket enclosing the wadding and trim with a frill around the top.
6 The lid is a rectangle with the embroidered panel set into it. A frill has been added around the edge with a tie at each end. The lid has been padded with polyester wadding and lined with another rectangle of cotton lawn.

WISTERIA

	DMC	Anchor	Appleton
Dark green	937	268	256
Light green	581	280	253
Light lilac	3042	870	101
Dark lilac	3041	871	103
Optional outlines			
Flowers	3740	872	104
Leaves and stems	937	268	256

DMC/Anchor

- 937/268
- 581/280
- 3042/870
- 3041/871
- 3740/872
- 937/268
- ☆ Centre stitch

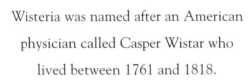

Originally from China and Japan, wisteria
is in the same family as the laburnum.
The roots and bark of the Chinese
wisteria are poisonous.

If your wisteria does not flower,
sparrows could be to blame. They are
particularly partial to the buds!

Wisteria was named after an American
physician called Casper Wistar who
lived between 1761 and 1818.

*Decorated layette basket with wisteria cross
stitch panel lid.*

XERANTHEMUM

Xeranthemums have pretty, daisy-like flowers with attractive, almost straw-like textured petals on long, wiry stems and are great favourites for dried flower arrangements.

Cheerfulness under adversity

Cross Stitch Project Folder

Think of all the hours spent on a project before it is finished – it deserves to be kept in something as attractive as this.

Design size: 6½ x 3½in (16 x 9cm)
Stitch count: 93 x 48

YOU WILL NEED

10 x 8in (25 x 20cm) 28-count cream linen
Stranded cotton (floss) as listed on the chart on page 100
Size 26 tapestry needle
24in (60cm) printed cotton fabric
24in (60cm) plain fabric for lining
2¾yd (2.5m) satin bias binding
12 x 24 inches (30 x 60 cm) polyester wadding

Stitches: Cross stitch, backstitch
Threads: Use two strands of stranded cotton (floss) for the cross stitch and one strand for the backstitch outline

1 Prepare your fabric (see page 112).
2 Following the chart on page 100 and starting at the centre, stitch the xeranthemum.
3 When complete, press (see page 113) and make up (see page 123 and below).
4 This folder is made up in exactly the same way as the make-up purses shown on page 109, with the cross stitch panel set into the front. The finished measurements of this one are 8 x 12in (20 x 30cm). If you want to make it larger or smaller, adjust the fabric quantities accordingly.
5 Add a strip of printed fabric to the inside of the front flap with satin binding loops caught under it. On to each of these loops, thread small brass curtain rings to act as thread organisers (see picture on page 124).

Xeranthemum

DMC/Anchor

◢◣	315/896
⊡	316/969
⊠	3041/871
− −	3042/870
H H	676/891
△ △	520/862
∧ ∧	522/860
——	934/862
═══	522/860
——	520/862
☆	Centre stitch

XERANTHEMUM

	DMC	Anchor	Appleton
Dark pink	315	896	715
Light pink	316	969	712
Dark violet	3041	871	103
Light violet	3042	870	101
Yellow	676	891	693
Dark green	520	862	295
Light green	522	860	292
Optional outlines			
Leaves and stems	934	862	407
Flower centre	522	860	292
Flower bases	520	862	295

Commonly known as straw flowers,
they originated in the Mediterranean and
south western Australia.

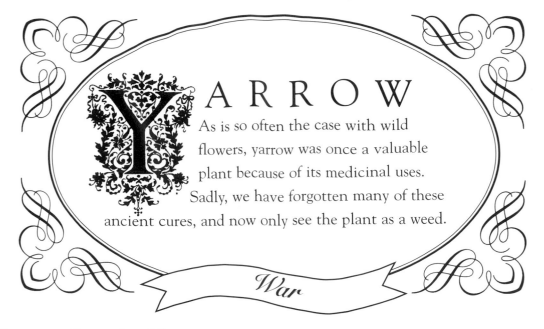

YARROW

As is so often the case with wild flowers, yarrow was once a valuable plant because of its medicinal uses. Sadly, we have forgotten many of these ancient cures, and now only see the plant as a weed.

War

Cross Stitch Picture

The yarrow seemed to have the same feel as the nettle (urtica) so I mounted and framed them exactly the same way to make a pair (pictured on page 87).

Design size: 5¹⁄₂ x 4in (14 x 10cm)
Stitch count: 82 x 60

YOU WILL NEED

12 x 10in (30 x 25cm) 28-count natural linen
Stranded cotton (floss) as listed on the chart on page 102
Size 26 tapestry needle
Dark green silk dupion for covering mount (optional)
Polyester wadding for padding

Stitches: Cross stitch, backstitch, French knots
Threads: Use two strands of stranded cotton (floss) for the cross stitch and French knots, and one strand for the backstitch outline

1 Prepare your fabric (see page 112).
2 Following the chart on page 102 and starting at the centre, stitch the yarrow. Add a small cluster of French knots in yellow on the yellow cross stitch in the centre of each flower.
3 Choose an alphabet (see page 106) for the name.
4 When complete, press (see page 113). Make a covered mount (see page 121) and frame as required.

'I will pick the green yarrow

– that my figure may be fuller,

– that my voice will be sweeter,

– that my lips will be like the juice of the

strawberry,

I shall wound every man, but no man shall

harm me'

An old Gaelic chant to be sung by a woman.

101

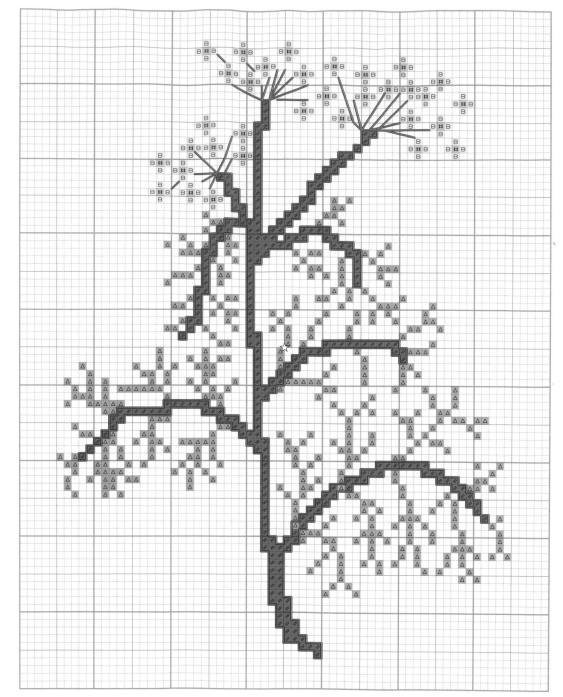

DMC/Anchor

B B		822/390
H H		676/891
		936/846
△ △		732/281
——		936/256
☆		Centre stitch

YARROW

	DMC	Anchor	Appleton
Cream	822	390	882
Yellow	676	891	693
Dark green	936	846	256
Light green	732	281	254
French knots	676	891	693
Optional outlines			
Stems	936	846	256

Common name – woundwort, because of its excellent properties for quelling bleeding. For this reason it was held in great esteem by the ancients and the Greek warrior Achilles was said to have used yarrow to heal the wounds made by iron weapons in battle.

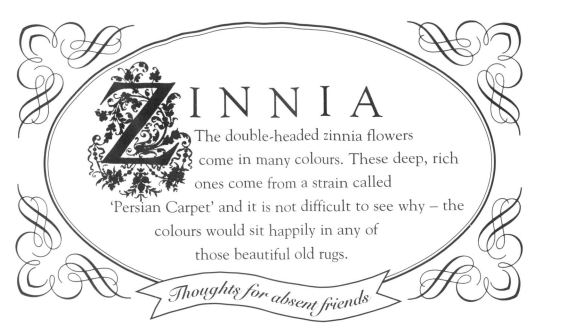

ZINNIA

The double-headed zinnia flowers come in many colours. These deep, rich ones come from a strain called 'Persian Carpet' and it is not difficult to see why – the colours would sit happily in any of those beautiful old rugs.

Thoughts for absent friends

Cross Stitch Picture

Pretty though it would look in a plain frame, this cross stitch picture looks even lovelier in a matching fabric-covered mount with a twisted cord trim.

Design size: 4¹⁄₂ x 3¹⁄₂in (11 x 9cm)
Stitch count: 60 x 47

YOU WILL NEED

10in (25cm) square, 28-count natural linen
Stranded cotton (floss) as listed on the chart on page 104
Size 26 tapestry needle
Fabric for making a covered mount
Polyester wadding for padding

Stitches: Cross stitch, backstitch, French knots
Threads: Use two strands of stranded cotton (floss) for the cross stitch and French knots, one strand for the backstitch outline

1 Prepare your fabric (see page 112).
2 Following the chart on page 104 and starting at the centre, stitch the zinnias. Add a cluster of French knots in orange on the orange cross stitch in the centre of each flower.
3 When complete, press (see page 113). Make a covered mount (see page 121) and a twisted cord (see page 125). Frame as required. I attached the cord using tiny dabs of general purpose adhesive. You may prefer to stitch it on with a needle and thread.

Despite their South American origins, zinnias were named after Johann Gottfried Zinn (1727–59), a German botanist and physician.

DMC/Anchor

▲▲	815/22
ИИ	Ecru/387
◢◢	3777/20
••	742/303
НН	977/313
△△	937/268
--	470/266
——	3371/382
——	937/268
☆	Centre stitch

ZINNIA

	DMC	Anchor	Appleton
Dark pink red	815	22	227
Ecru	Ecru	387	882
Red	3777	20	725
Gold	742	303	474
Orange	977	313	862
Dark green	937	268	254
Light green	470	266	253
Optional outlines			
Flowers	3371	382	588
Leaves and stems	937	268	254

These bright blooms originally came

from South America.

Opposite: *Zinnia cross stitch picture.*

104

Alphabets and Borders

This last section contains all the alphabets and the twisted border that I have used to complete the projects. They can all be used in combination with each other and you could use them to personalize your work, with friends' names and dates as well as the names of the flowers. In the pictures (below and on page 109) you can see five projects that I have stitched using only the alphabets. They are all very quick and easy little projects to do but make delightful gifts to receive.

The birthday card and cake band have only very small amounts of stitching on them but would both be a pleasure to give or receive.

The make-up purses have a trimming of antique lace; one uses space-dyed stranded cotton (floss) and on the other each letter is a different shade to pick out the colours of the Liberty lawn fabrics.

The little wedding ring purse is made in silk dupion trimmed with lace and would make a very pretty keepsake for a bride.

Birthday cake band (left) and card (right).

106

ABCDE
FGHIJK
LMNOP
QRSTU
VWXYZ

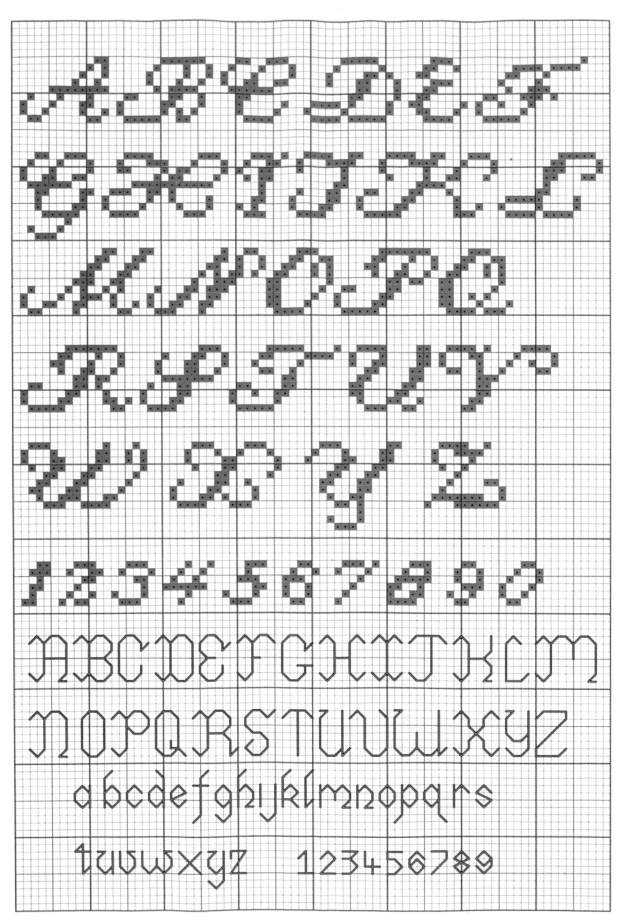

From top to bottom: *Two named make-up purses and wedding ring purse.*

109

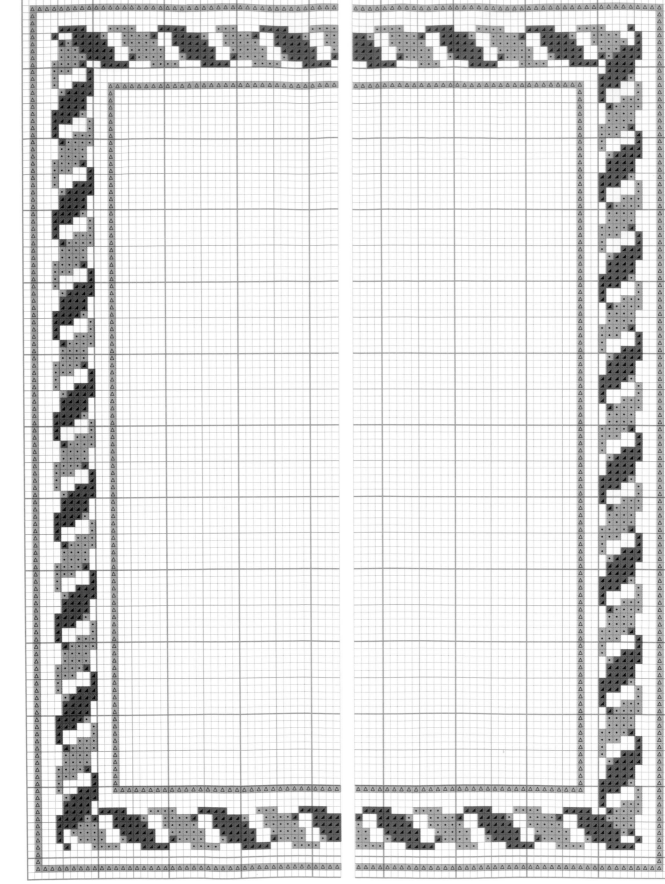

Materials and Techniques

Cross Stitch

FABRICS

The two most commonly used fabrics for cross stitch are Aida and linen. Nearly all the designs in this book are stitched on linen because it is my personal favourite, but in no way should that stop you using Aida if you are more comfortable with it. Aida is woven in blocks and is an extremely good fabric for a beginner as it is very easy to count – one stitch is worked over one block. Linen is worked over two threads in each direction (see single cross stitch, page 112). Having said that, the difference between working on Aida and linen really boils down to the difference between counting to one or to two, so maybe if you can count to two you should give it a go if you have been shy of it until now!

The fabrics used for cross stitch are all evenweave. This means that they have the same number of threads or blocks per inch in both the length and width of the fabric. So any cross stitch made on the fabric, either over two threads or one block, will always be square.

The thread count of a fabric tells how many threads or blocks there are per inch. Fabrics come in a range of different counts, but the most frequently used are 28-count linen and its equivalent 14-count Aida; in both cases you work 14 stitches to the inch. There are also several cotton and cotton-mixture evenweave fabrics available, the most recent of which is Jobelan, remarkable for the huge selection of colours and several different counts in the range.

You can use any of the charts in this book on any type of evenweave fabric; just use the stitch counts given to calculate the dimensions of the finished design (see page 112) and choose the size most suited to the particular project that you have in mind.

THREADS

All the cross stitch designs in this book have been stitched using DMC stranded cotton (floss). I have quoted alternative Anchor numbers but these are only a close match and will not necessarily give an identical result. When selecting threads always have the fabric that you intend stitching on with you, as it may affect your choice. There is no law that says you have to use the same threads as on the chart – you may prefer to change some.

NEEDLES

You will need tapestry needles with a blunt end for cross stitch. The most commonly used sizes are 24 and 26 (26 being the finer). Try the needle through the fabric that you are going to use; it should pass easily through but there should be some slight resistance so that it does not fall through. Gold-plated and, more recently, platinum-plated needles are available. They are very smooth because of their precious plating and are a pleasure to stitch with. If you have not yet tried them I recommend you give yourself a treat.

FRAMES AND HOOPS

It is not necessary to use a frame or hoop for cross stitch, but if you find it makes working easier use a hoop for small pieces and a rectangular frame for larger pieces. If you use a hoop ensure that all the design is well within its stitching area. Do not try to fit it over worked areas as it may damage your stitches and will not work well over the thickness of the embroidery. In a rectangular frame, the fabric is stitched to webbing along the width of the frame and laced to the side bars. Excess fabric is taken up by rollers at the top and bottom.

Embroidery hoop.

THE CHARTS

Each square on the chart represents two threads of linen (see page 112 for stitching over two threads of linen) or one block of Aida. Each occupied square represents one stitch on the fabric. Backstitch outlines are represented by a solid line. Use the key to tell you what colour each stitch or backstitch should be. Outlining the details on the designs is optional; but if you decide to outline, this must be done last, when all the cross stitching is complete.

CALCULATING THE DESIGN SIZE

Stitch counts are given for all the designs in this book. These are the maximum number of stitches in each direction. Divide these numbers by the number of stitches to the inch of your chosen fabric and this will give you the size of the design in inches on that particular fabric.

For example, for a stitch count of 84 x 42 on 28-count linen (14 stitches per inch):
Design size = stitch count/stitches per inch
84/14 = 6in; 42/14 = 3in
Design size on 28-count fabric = 6 x 3in

It is important to check the thread count and stitch count before you start a project if it is to fit a certain frame size.

WHERE TO START

When cutting the fabric, allow at least 6in (15cm) extra to the completed dimension on both the length and width. This will leave at least a 3in (7.5cm) unstitched margin for stretching and mounting. Allow more on larger designs. If you are in any doubt as to how you intend to mount your work allow plenty of space around the design so that you can decide as you work.

Fold the fabric in four to find the centre and then work a line of tacking (basting) stitches following the threads to mark both folds. These will cross in the middle of the fabric and this is where you should start stitching from the middle of the chart, which is also marked; then your design will always be centred. Sew a narrow hem or oversew to prevent fraying and you are ready to stitch.

STARTING AND FINISHING

There are two methods of starting cross stitch: the waste knot method and the looped start. The looped start is the easiest and neatest, but you can only use it when you are stitching with an even number of strands. To stitch with two strands take a single thread that is twice the length that you need, fold it in half and thread the two ends through the needle leaving the loop at the other end. Push the needle up through the fabric with your first stitch and down again leaving the loop hanging at the back of the fabric. Now pass the needle through the loop thus anchoring the thread.

If you are using the waste knot method to start, you can have any number of strands in your needle. Tie a knot in the end of the thread and pull the thread through your fabric about one inch from where you intend to begin stitching, leaving the knot on the top of the fabric. Work your cross stitches back towards

the knot catching the starting thread in the back of the stitches. When you reach the knot, cut it off.

To finish off an area of cross stitch, run the needle through a few stitches on the back of your work and cut the end of the thread off close to the stitching. Do not run a dark colour through lighter stitches as it may show through.

THE STITCHES

A cross stitch has two parts and can be worked in one of two ways. A complete stitch can be worked at once or a number of half cross stitches can be worked in a row and then crossed on the return journey. The only rule is that all the top stitches of the whole piece of the work must lie in the same direction. Any that do not will catch the light and annoy you forever once the finished piece hangs on the wall.

SINGLE CROSS STITCH

A cross stitch on linen is shown below, worked over two threads. The two diagonals are worked one after the other to make a cross.

A ROW OF CROSS STITCH

If you are working an area of cross stitch in one colour, you may find it easier to use the method shown here. A row of half cross stitches are made and then crossed on the return.

BACKSTITCH OUTLINE
Always work the design before outlining using the simple stitch shown below.

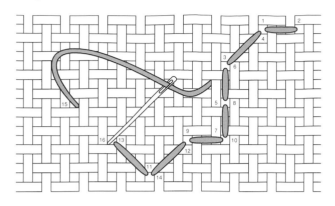

FRENCH KNOTS
Bring your needle up through the fabric, hold the thread taut and wind the needle once around the thread. Pull the twist down on to the surface of the fabric and insert the needle into almost the same place as it came out (but not quite or your knot will disappear through the hole). Pull the needle carefully through the fabric still keeping tension on the thread until you have to let go. If you take the thread around the needle more than once you will tend to get a looser-looking knot. If you want a larger knot use more strands of your thread.

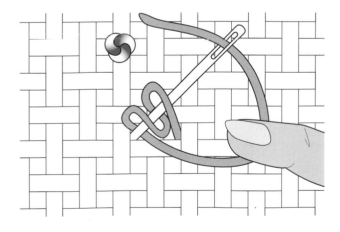

WASHING
It is advisable to wash cross stitch once you have completed the stitching. Reputable makes of thread should be colour-fast but if you are in doubt dampen some thread and blot it on tissue. If there is any trace of colour on the tissue do not wash. Washing with a gentle, bleach-free soap product will freshen the piece. Rinse well in hand-hot water and lay on a towel. Roll the towel and embroidery to remove excess moisture and then allow to dry naturally.

PRESSING
If your piece is fairly small, ironing should be sufficient to remove creases. Heat the iron to a hot setting, cover the ironing board with two layers of towelling and place the embroidery face down on top, with the back of the work towards you. Press firmly using plenty of steam. If you do not have a steam iron, cover the back of the work with a damp cloth and press your embroidery through the cloth. Never press cross stitch on the right side. Leave the embroidery to cool and dry before framing or making up.

If you have worked a large piece on linen and have trouble removing the creases you will find that it is well worth stretching on a board – your embroidery will be beautifully flat and the linen will seem like new. Follow the instructions for stretching crewelwork on page 120.

Canvaswork

CANVAS
Canvas is available in two main types: single thread, or mono canvas; and double thread, or Penelope canvas. Most of the canvaswork projects in this book are worked on interlock mono canvas, where the threads along the length are in fact double threads twisted together to hold the cross threads firmly in place. This produces a more stable canvas, ideal for working designs that include long stitches which might otherwise pull loose canvas threads together and so make holes in your work. The disadvantage of interlock canvas is that it is only available in white. Do not stitch too tightly or the canvas will show through.

Canvas is most commonly available in four thread counts. The table below shows you how many strands of Appleton crewel wool (yarn) and what size needle you should use for each gauge. You can use any of the charts in this book with any gauge of canvas; just use the stitch counts given to calculate the dimensions of the finished design (see page 112) and choose the size most suited to the project that you have in mind.

Canvas gauge	Strands of crewel wool (yarn)	Size of needle
Threads per inch	Working in tent stitch	
10	6	20
12	4	20
14	3	22
18	2	22 or 24

THREADS

Crewel wool (yarn) is a fine, twisted, two-ply yarn which may be used singly or as two or more strands in the needle. When several strands are used in this way the wool (yarn) lies flat and covers the threads of the canvas better. If you are a particularly tight stitcher do add in an extra strand to achieve a good cover. This is also a good idea if you are working any design that involves a lot of long stitches when you will often find that the canvas shows through more readily. I have used Appleton's crewel wool (yarn) throughout the book because the colour range is so large and each colour is then produced in a carefully graded range of shades. There is a very wide variety of yarns and threads on the market and all stitchers seem to have their own particular favourites. If you have just discovered a new and tempting thread, do experiment using the charts given in this book.

NEEDLES

Tapestry needles are blunt so that they pass through the canvas without catching. The size required will vary according to the number of strands that you are using and the gauge of canvas you have chosen (see the chart on page 113 for more details). The needle when threaded should pass easily through the canvas. You should not have to tug it too much otherwise the yarn will wear as it passes through the eye of the needle. As you stitch move the needle along the yarn so that the same place is not pulled through the canvas. You will find that as you stitch your yarn will become twisted; drop the needle every now and again and let it hang freely to allow the yarn to untwist. Do treat yourself to a gold-plated needle for canvaswork it will never tarnish and will always be a pleasure to use.

EMBROIDERY FRAMES

At the risk of being shot down in flames by the more traditional needlewomen amongst us, I have to say that the use of a frame for canvaswork is a matter of personal preference! I certainly recommend using one for any design which involves long stitches – as do all the woolwork projects in this book – or which requires careful counting from a chart. For lots of the projects in this book I worked the design or motif on a frame and then filled in the background with the canvas in my hand. If you do work in the hand you should roll the canvas rather than scrunch it up and, of course, you will need to stretch the finished piece carefully as it distorts more than when it has been worked on a frame.

There are many types of frames available and you should choose the one that you are most comfortable with and that fits your budget. Follow the manufacturer's instructions for mounting the canvas.

Never use an embroidery hoop on canvas unless you have one that is big enough to contain the entire worked area. Where the canvas has been stretched tightly between the rings it will become distorted, and if this distortion is then stitched over there will be a shadow in the embroidery which often remains, even after stretching.

THE CHARTS AND COLOURED LINE DRAWINGS

Charts for cross stitch can also be used for canvaswork, usually working tent stitch in wool (yarn). Each occupied square represents one stitch of the design, and the unoccupied squares represent the background which, on canvas, has to be stitched as well. If a background colour is not suggested, choose one that is suitable and decide on the extent of the background area to be covered. The Rose Velvet-backed Canvaswork Pincusion on page 74 uses this approach. You can work any of the cross stitch charts in this book on canvas, using wool (yarn) instead of stranded cotton (floss).

Most of the canvaswork projects in this book, however, use not only tent stitch but also stitches that are more traditional to crewelwork, such as long and short stitch, split backstitch and French knots, I have used the term 'woolwork' for this technique. Because they make use of these more freely formed stitches, it is not appropriate to work from a counted stitch chart. What you need to do, therefore, is trace the coloured line drawing from the relevant page of this book, transfer the outline on to the canvas and stitch in much the same way as for crewelwork on fabric. The chart, the photograph of the finished piece and the colouring of the line drawing all help in placing colour accurately.

WHERE TO START

When cutting the canvas, allow at least 6in (15cm) extra to the completed dimension on both the length and width. This amount will leave at least a 3in (7.5cm) unstitched margin all around the embroidery for stretching and mounting.

Bind the edge of your canvas with masking tape before you begin to stitch. Not only will this protect your hands, but it will also prevent the yarns from catching on the rough edge where the threads have been cut.

Trace the outline of the design on to the canvas (see opposite). Read 'General Working Advice', on page 116, and follow the individual project steps for more detailed instructions. Once the design has been completed, draw a pencil line on the canvas to mark out the extent of the total background area before you begin to fill in.

TRACING THE OUTLINE ON TO CANVAS

YOU WILL NEED

A black waterproof felt tip pen
A sheet of tracing paper
Masking tape

1 First, trace the outline of the crewel design on to tracing paper. (You could work straight from the page of the book, but when you lay the canvas over and draw the ink will mark the book and spoil it.)

2 To make some designs suitable for stitching with three strands of wool (yarn) on canvas I enlarged their tracings by 140% on a photocopier. The instructions for individual projects will tell you whether to enlarge the drawing or not.

3 Place the outline tracing on a flat surface and secure it with masking tape. Lay the square of canvas centrally over the drawing and secure with masking tape. Using the waterproof pen draw all the lines that you will be able to see quite clearly through the canvas. It is very important that the pen is waterproof so that when you stretch the finished piece the ink will not run and spoil your embroidery.

STARTING AND FINISHING

To begin with a waste knot, start by knotting the end of the yarn and pulling it through your canvas about an inch from where you intend to begin stitching, leaving the knot on the top. Work your stitches towards the knot catching the starting yarn into the back of the stitches. When you reach the knot cut it off. Once you have some completed stitching on the canvas you can run the yarn under a few stitches on the back to begin a new length of yarn or a new colour. Do this carefully so that you do not alter the tension of the existing stitches on the front of the canvas. As with cross stitch, you can use a looped start for canvaswork if you are working with an even number of threads. The method is described on page 112.

To finish off, run the needle through a few stitches on the back of your work and cut the end of the yarn off close to the stitching, again take care not to alter your tension. Do not run a dark colour through lighter stitches as it may show through to the front of the fabric.

THE STITCHES

These are the basic stitches used in canvaswork. For some of the projects you will also need to refer to the crewelwork stitches on page 118, as some of the stitching is a combination of canvaswork and simple crewelwork, for example the Anemone Pillow, page 10.

TENT STITCH

There are two methods of working tent stitch: diagonal, as shown below (top); and continental, as shown below (bottom). Diagonal tent stitch distorts the canvas less, so use it wherever possible, especially when you are working backgrounds.

LONG LEGGED CROSS STITCH

Four threads forwards and two threads back as you work the stitch. This gives a plaited braid effect which is useful for finishing off around a tent stitch square.

BACKSTITCH OUTLINE

Worked with tent stitch to enhance details. Always work the design and any surrounding background

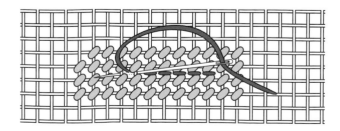

115

before the outlining which will not show unless it sits on top of the tent stitch. Use only one, or possibly two, strands of crewel wool (yarn) depending on the size of the tent stitch

GENERAL WORKING ADVICE

Each project gives details of which stitches and which colours to use. However, the following instructions apply in general.

1 The basic stitch is long and short stitch with which you can shade and blend colours. Work into every canvas hole around the edges of a shape but change the direction of the stitches as you work your way around leaves and petals by overlapping in the centre (see page 118). You will find it easier to come up through the canvas on the outside and down towards the centre. Work subsequent rows from the centre outwards. A long stitch should alternate with a short one but do not be too rigid about this.

2 When working long and short stitch always split the threads of each successive layer of stitching to ensure a good colour blend and smooth stitches.

3 As you work, be aware of the direction of each thread that you lay on the canvas, making sure the stitches of the next layer lie in the same direction as the first. As a general rule, try to stitch the design in the direction the plant would grow in – you will obtain a much better result.

4 Take great care with the direction of each stitch as you work so that they all seem to radiate out from the centre of the leaf or flower. Overlap (or underlap) some stitches towards the centre to achieve this.

5 Your stitches should be longer than feels necessary because they will be shortened by the following layer of stitches.

6 Work features such as veins over the top of the stitched flower. As you will have covered the original lines with stitching, use the photograph and drawing to help you get the positions right.

STRETCHING AND STARCHING

It is in the nature of canvaswork to distort as it is worked, particularly when using tent stitch. Even if you have worked on a frame and you think your embroidery is square you should still stretch and starch – you will be surprised how much the appearance is improved. Not only will the piece be perfectly square but the tension of the stitching will become more even. If you are tempted to miss out this vital stage between the stitching and the making up of your project it will never look as good as it might.

YOU WILL NEED

A large, flat, clean board (chipboard is ideal)
A sheet of dressmaker's graph paper (marked in 1cm squares)
Plenty of 1in nails. A hammer
Cold water starch (most easily available as wallpaper paste. Make sure that you buy a brand without plasticiser. I always use a brand called Lap which is widely available)
Masking tape
A kitchen palette knife (one with a rubber blade is ideal)

1 Cover the board with the sheet of squared paper and secure with masking tape around the edge.
2 Place the embroidery, right side down, on top of the squared paper. You will be able to see the squares of the paper through the unstitched margin of the canvas. Begin nailing in one corner about 2in (5cm) away from the embroidery. Hammer the nails in just far enough to hold firmly in the board. Follow one line of holes in the canvas and nail into every second intersection of a line in the paper. It is important to keep the nails no more than ³⁄₄in (2cm) apart or the edge of the embroidery will not be straight.
3 When you have completed the first side, go back to the corner and repeat for the side at right angles to it.
4 Draw the pencil line in the canvas line from the last nail on each side to cross at the corner diagonally opposite to the one you started from. Lift the canvas and using the squares find the position on the paper where the lines cross from the nailed corners; this is where the last corner of the canvas must be stretched to. If your work is badly distorted it will help to dampen the embroidery at this stage.
5 Pull out the embroidery, nail this last corner and then finish nailing the last two sides.
6 Mix a small quantity of paste to the consistency of soft butter and, using the palette knife, spread it evenly but sparingly over the back of the embroidery. Try not to let the starch go over the edges of the embroidery as it will stick the work to the paper and spoil the board for future use. Allow to dry naturally and completely.
7 Remove the nails and turn the embroidery over to reveal a beautiful squared and even piece of work.

Crewelwork

FABRICS

The crewelwork designs in this book are all worked on fine linen union. There are many other suitable fabrics on the market and the choice is much wider than for counted embroidery as the fabric need not be of an evenweave. Your chosen fabric should have a close weave, so that the threads will not separate when you stitch, and be of medium weight. Some of the finer counts of evenweave linen are also suitable for crewelwork. Ask your local embroidery shop for a fabric suitable for surface embroidery if you are in doubt. Don't be afraid to try any fabric for crewelwork if you like the look and colour of it.

One word of advice, however: I do advise you to stick to natural fibres rather than using synthetic ones. Finally, the colour of the background fabric you use is up to you, but do try it with the thread colours you intend to use before you buy.

THREADS

The dictionary defines crewel as 'a loosely twisted worsted yarn used in embroidery' and so traditionally crewelwork has always been done using crewel wool yarn. There are several types on the market; I have chosen Appleton's crewel wool (yarn) because of its availability and superb colour range. If you particularly want to use another type use the colourings of the line drawings of the various flowers to help you choose a suitable set of shades in your chosen brand; alternatively, you can use stranded cotton (floss) as you can see in the Fritillary on the base of the etui on page 27.

NEEDLES

Crewel needles have sharp points and long eyes for easy threading. They come in a wide range of sizes, the most useful being 7 and 5 (7 being finer than 5). Really, the finer the needle the better for crewel embroidery, but be guided by how easily you can thread your needle, and change the size accordingly. Crewel needles are now also available gold-plated and you will especially notice the advantage of the smoothness of gold when working this type of embroidery.

EMBROIDERY FRAMES AND HOOPS

Always use a frame or hoop when doing crewel embroidery. It is very important to keep the fabric taut as some of the stitches used in crewelwork are quite long and it is easy to bunch up the fabric if it is not held tight.

If you decide to use a rectangular frame, which you will need for a larger design, they come in a variety of sizes and types. The fabric is stitched to webbing along the width of the frame and laced to the side bars. Excess fabric is taken up by rollers at the top and bottom. If you use a hoop ensure that all the design is well within its stitching area.

Do not try to fit it over worked areas as it may damage your stitches and will not work well over the thickness of the embroidery.

THE COLOURED LINE DRAWINGS

The colouring of these drawings is only a guide as to where to stitch the different coloured yarns – crewelwork is a free form of embroidery and you will have to make some decisions for yourself. The photograph of the finished piece is always a good reference for shading, the chart for each design will show which colours are used in which areas, and the step-by-step instructions take you through which colour to use where. Please do not be frightened by the absence of any lines to follow; once you start you will be surprised at how easy it is, and how creative you can be!

There is a coloured drawing for every flower in the book; but only some flowers have detailed instructions for crewelwork. The idea is that once you have worked through projects with detailed instructions you will know how to attempt crewelwork embroidery, and will be able to stitch all the flowers in the alphabet. So, if you have not tried this type of embroidery before, start by working one of the crewel miniatures which is small and has detailed instructions. Then stitch some of the larger projects which have detailed instructions before attempting one of the flowers that is not shown stitched.

WHERE TO START

When cutting your fabric you should allow at least 6in (15cm) extra to the completed dimension on both the length and width. This will leave at least a 3in (7.5cm) border for stretching and mounting. For a large design you should allow more, and if you are in any doubt as to how you intend to mount your work allow plenty of space around the design while you decide as you work.

To prevent fraying, work a narrow hem around the edge of your fabric or bind the edge with masking tape before you begin to stitch. Trace the outline of the design on to the fabric (see below) and mount into a hoop or frame.

TRACING AN OUTLINE ON TO FABRIC

YOU WILL NEED

A black felt tip pen
A water soluble pen
A sheet of tracing paper
Masking tape

1 First, trace the outline on to tracing paper using the black felt tip pen. (You could work straight from the page of the book but you might mark the book and spoil it.)
2 I used an artist's light box to trace the outlines on

to the fabric, but if one is not available to you use daylight as your source of light by taping your tracing of the outline to a window pane and then taping the square of linen over it. (Some photographic slide viewers also work well for this.) The outline will show through the fabric and you will be able to trace it using the water soluble pen.

STARTING AND FINISHING

You can start your stitching using a waste knot as with cross stitch, but it is not as easy to stitch towards the knot in crewelwork. You may prefer to do as I do and leave the knot on the top of the fabric about four inches from where you intend to start stitching. Once there is enough stitching on the fabric cut the knot off and thread the four inch length in the needle and work into the back of the fabric.

To begin and finish off after this you can just run the yarn through the back of the stitching that you have already completed on the fabric.

THE STITCHES

For some of the projects in this book you will need to refer to this page as well as to the canvaswork stitches on page 115, as woolwork is a combination of canvas and simple crewelwork.

SPLIT BACKSTITCH

Similar to backstitch, except that the needle is inserted into the previous stitch; take care to actually split the thread.

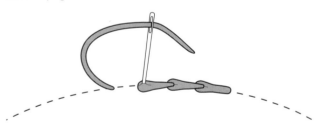

LONG AND SHORT STITCH

Only the first row worked has long and short stitches; following rows are all long. Begin at the outside edge

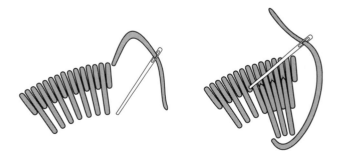

and then stitch the following rows into the stitches already worked, splitting the threads to blend the stitches and colours. Do not be afraid to make the stitches longer than you feel you should, as they will be shortened by the next layer of stitching. Do not try to follow this diagram too rigidly – use it as a guide only because you will have to adapt to the shape that you have to fill.

STEM STITCH

Hold the thread down with your finger each time you make a stitch to keep it out of the way and also to maintain an even tension.

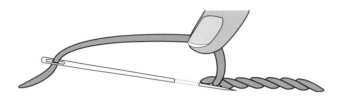

SATIN STITCH

These are simply straight flat stitches laid side by side, although the length of each stitch may vary from its neighbours to fill the shape, of a petal or leaf for example. Always come up the same side and down on the other so that you cover the back of the fabric as well. This way your stitches will lie closely beside each other.

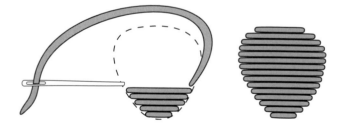

FRENCH KNOTS

Bring your needle up through the fabric, hold the thread taut and wind the needle once around the thread. Pull the twist down on to the surface of the fabric and insert the needle into almost the same place as it came out (but not quite or your knot will disappear through the hole). Pull the needle carefully through the fabric still keeping tension on the thread until you have to let go. If you take the thread around the needle more than once you will tend to get a looser-looking knot. If you want a larger knot use more strands of your thread.

BULLION KNOTS

The length of the finished coil of a bullion knot is determined by the length of the first stitch you make. Wind the thread around the needle several times until the length of the coil equals the length of the first stitch. Hold the thread coil and needle between your thumb and finger and gently but firmly pull the needle through. Allow the coil to turn back on itself and push the needle through to the back of the fabric.

Below: *Create a blended effect with backstitch and long and short stitch.*

GENERAL WORKING ADVICE

Each project gives details of which stitches and which colours to use. However, the following intructions apply in general.

1 The basic stitch is long and short stitch with which you can shade and blend colours. Stitch the outlines of the design in split backstitch in the appropriate colour, then work long and short stitch over the top (page 118). This gives a slightly raised effect to the edges of the leaves and petals, and a good edge to the long and short stitch.

2 Begin the long and short stitch, you will find it easier to come up through the fabric on the outside and down towards the centre. Work subsequent rows from the centre outwards. A long stitch should alternate with a short one but do not be too rigid about this. When working long and short stitch always split the threads of each successive layer of stitching to

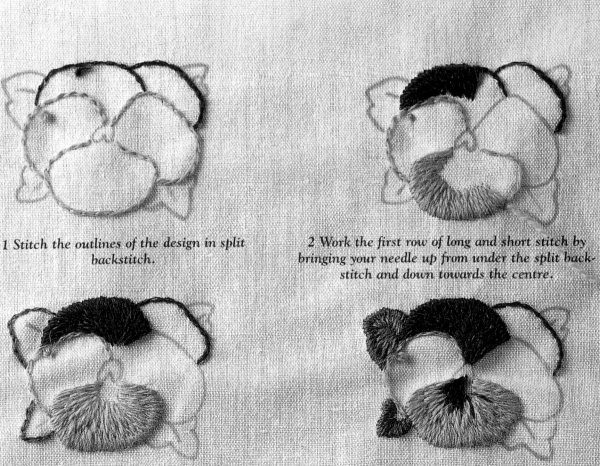

1 Stitch the outlines of the design in split backstitch.

2 Work the first row of long and short stitch by bringing your needle up from under the split backstitch and down towards the centre.

3 Work subsequent rows from the centre outwards.

4 Your stitches should appear to radiate out of the centre of the flower.

ensure a good blending of colour and smooth stitches. Your stitches should be longer than feels necessary because they will be shortened by the following layer of stitches.

3 As you work, be aware of the direction of each thread that you lay on the canvas, making sure the stitches of the next layer lie in the same direction as the first. As a general rule, try to stitch the design in the direction the plant would grow in – you will obtain a much better result. Take great care with the direction of each stitch as you work so that they all seem to radiate out from the centre of the leaf or flower. You will have to overlap (or underlap) some towards the centre to achieve this.

4 Work features such as veins over the top of the stitched flower. As you will have covered the original lines with stitching, use the photograph and drawing to help you get the positions right.

WASHING

It is advisable to wash crewelwork once you have completed the stitching. If you have used the tracing method described in the text you will need to rinse away the water soluble pen lines, also washing with a gentle, bleach-free soap product will freshen the piece. Rinse well in hand-hot water and lay on a towel. Roll up the towel tightly with the embroidery in it to remove the excess moisture and then allow to dry naturally.

PRESSING

If your piece is fairly small, ironing should be sufficient to remove creases and puckers caused by the stitching. If your work is very puckered or quite large you may need to stretch it (see next section). Heat the iron to a hot setting, cover the ironing board with two layers of towelling and place the embroidery, face down with the back of the work towards you, on the towelling. Press firmly using plenty of steam. If you do not have a steam iron, cover the back of the work with a damp cloth and press your embroidery through the cloth. Never press crewelwork on the right side. Leave the embroidery to cool and dry before framing or making up.

STRETCHING

If you have completed a large piece of crewelwork, or have tried ironing as above and are not satisfied, you will need to stretch your embroidery. This will remove any puckers that are within the embroidered area and are difficult to iron out. If you are in doubt as to which method to use, choose this one; although it takes longer it always works.

The method is similar to that used for canvaswork, but instead of covering the back of the nailed-out embroidery with paste, nail it face up and dampen with water from a spray (available from garden centres for spraying house plants) filled with tap water. Do not worry if the fabric seems to stretch and go loose on the nails; it will tighten as it dries. Allow to dry completely and remove the nails.

Beading

Beading is a very simple technique that can be used to work a complete design (see the Ivy Christmas Card, page 38) or to add detail to a piece (see the Beaded Sunflower Pillow, page 76). It was very popular with the Victorians, and has recently been revived with great success.

BEADS, NEEDLES AND THREADS

The tiny beads used in embroidery are now easy to buy. Mill Hill beads, for example, produce an incredible range of colours and types (see Suppliers, page 126). However, there is nothing stopping you searching in second-hand shops and jumble sales for old necklaces made from tiny beads, and using them for your embroidery. Not only will they be a treasured find, they may even be Victorian as well!

Such tiny beads need very fine needles. The best to use are special beading needles which are very long and fine. Some people prefer to use shorter quilting needles. The only rule is – if you can thread a bead along the needle, then use it!

The best and strongest thread to attach beads with is sewing thread, though you could use doubled stranded cotton (floss).

FABRICS

The usual fabrics beads are applied to are Aida and linen, as beading is often used with cross stitch. Projects that are completely beaded will usually be worked on these fabrics, too. But beads can be applied to canvas as well. In fact, double thread canvas is very appropriate for beadwork as each set of double threads makes a cradle to support each bead and gives a much more even finish. They can also be attached over stitching such as tent stitch and cross stitch, and sit on the surface of the embroidery.

ATTACHING THE BEADS

Beads are attached with sewing thread, stitching a half cross stitch. Bring the needle up through the fabric, thread a bead on to it, then finish the half cross stitch. You will find that the beads sit neatly on the fabric and as you build up the design they form very even rows.

Making up the Projects

Mounting Ready For Framing

I like to use lightweight foam core as mounting board for embroidery. This is made of two sheets of card with a very thin layer of polystyrene inbetween. The layer of polystyrene makes it very easy to pin into the side edge of the board, and because it is light it is also very easy to cut to size with a blade and metal straight edge ruler.

There are two alternatives: either you can purchase a ready-made frame and cut the board to fit this; or you can mount the embroidery exactly as you want to and then have a frame custom-made to fit. Obviously, the first alternative will cost less but the second will probably give a better finish.

Once you have cut the board to the required size, lay the embroidery over it and centre it. If your embroidery has a border you can count threads to each edge and centre very accurately; but if not, do this by eye. Using ordinary dressmaker's pins, pin through the embroidery into the edge of the board following one thread of the fabric. If you pin each edge in the middle first and then work out towards the corners you will find it easy to achieve. Time and care taken at this stage is well spent and you should not carry on until you are quite happy that your embroidery is completely straight and evenly tensioned on the board.

When you are happy that your embroidery is properly fixed on to the mounting board, turn the board over and secure all of the excess fabric either with double-sided tape or by lacing across the back using strong thread.

You may notice that most of the framed projects in this book have been padded before framing. This is very easily done by cutting a piece of polyester wadding (batting) to exactly the same size as your mounting board and then attaching this wadding to the board with double-sided tape. Then pin your embroidery over the padded board in exactly the same way as described above.

A word of caution: you should only pad your embroidery in this way if you are mounting without glass or you will simply push the surface of the embroidery against the underside of the glass and flatten it. Also, take care if you are using a pre-cut or covered mount. If you pad the embroidery as well it will make the mount stick out.

Making a Covered Mount

Some frames come with a pre-cut mount and most framers will cut one for you. Alternatively, you can cut one for yourself if you have a steady hand with the craft knife.

Cover the mount with a layer of polyester wadding (batting) attached with double-sided tape. Lay your chosen fabric over it and pin the sides just as though there was no hole in the middle – follow the instructions in the last paragraph for 'Mounting Ready For Framing' – using double-sided tape to secure it. Take care to get the grain of the fabric straight and to get any patterns or motifs placed correctly.

Now cut out the central panel, leaving a ³/₄in (2cm) turn-in. If you are making a round-holed mount, clip the turn-in all around the hole; or clip corners on a square or oblong shape. These clips should be made nearly to the edge of the mount board but not quite. Now turn-in the edges and secure with double-sided tape.

Ribbon and Bow Hanger

1 To trim a 5in (13cm) round frame, make a ribbon strip to support the picture 2 x 11in (5 x 28cm) with points on one end. Attach a brass curtain ring to the top for hanging.
2 Make another strip 2 x 18in (5 x 45cm) and tie in a bow. Stitch the bow to the top of the hanger and then attach the frame with staples from behind. Alternatively, stitch the picture hook to the ribbon.

Inset Cushion with Mitred Corners
(piped or frilled)

FOR A PIPED EDGE
YOU WILL NEED
20in (50cm) furnishing fabric
2yd (180cm) No 3 piping cord
A cushion pad 1-2in (2.5-5cm) larger than the finished cushion

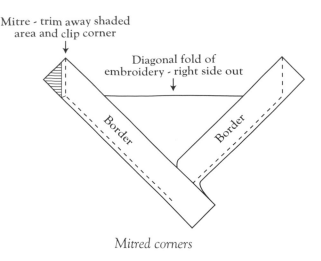

Mitred corners

*28in (70cm) fabric fine enough to be gathered easily
A cushion pad 1-2in (2.5-5cm) larger than the
finished cushion*

1 The seam allowance throughout is ¹/₂in (1.25cm). Measure the embroidery and decide on the size that you would like the finished cushion to be. Subtract the embroidery measurement from the finished measurement, divide this by two and add on two seam allowances. This gives you the total width for the border pieces.

2 Using either cutting plan below, cut all the pieces.

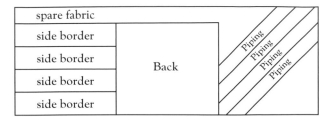

Cutting plan – piped version

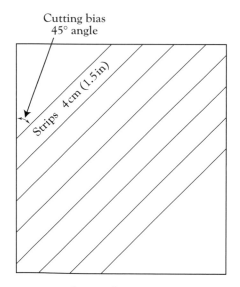

PIPED CUSHION

1 Cut enough bias strips 2in (5cm) wide to go round the cushion. It is important that these strips are on the true bias of the fabric and are cut at a 45 degree angle (see below). Stitch together enough bias strips to make the required length (see below, bottom).

Cutting plan – frilled version

3 Cut the embroidery to the required size plus ¹/₂in (1.25cm) seam allowances.

4 Find the mid point of each edge by folding, and mark it with a pin. Fold each border panel in half to find the centre point and mark with a pin.

5 Pin the border panels to the embroidery, matching the centre points, and leaving the ends free. Machine stitch these seams. The stitching of each side should meet at the corners exactly.

6 Fold the embroidery in half diagonally, wrong sides together, and mitre the corners by stitching a line from the corner of the embroidery to the corner of the border panels (see top right). Trim the excess cloth on these seams and clip the corners.

7 Repeat, folding on the other diagonal, to mitre the other two corners.

Cutting bias strips

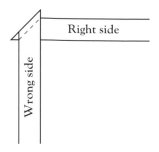

Joining bias strips

2 Fold the length in half and, using the piping foot of your sewing machine, carefully stitch the cord into the folded bias.

3 Using the piping foot, machine to the outer edge of the front, clipping the piping seam allowance at the corners as you go. To make a neat join in the piping when you reach the bottom edge, lay one end over the other and cut away the excess on each end leaving a ¹/₂in (1.25 cm) seam allowance.

4 Machine or hand stitch a straight seam. Trim the two ends of the cord so that they butt up to each other and then insert them back into the piping.

5 Finish attaching the embroidery to the piping across the join. Lay the back over the front, right sides together, and stitch, working tightly against the piping and leaving an opening at the bottom to insert the cushion pad.

6 Turn right sides out, insert the pad and slip stitch the opening to finish the cushion.

FRILLED CUSHION

1 Seam the frill pieces together to form a continuous loop and fold this in half, right sides out. Run gathers along the raw edges and pull up to fit the outer edge of the cushion.

2 Pin the frill to the edge of the front, spreading the gathers evenly, with the folded edges facing the centre of the cushion. Stitch this seam.

3 Pin the back to the front, right sides together. Stitch, leaving an opening to insert the cushion pad.

4 Turn right sides out, insert the pad and slip stitch the opening to finish the cushion.

Inset Cushion with Bows

YOU WILL NEED

20in (50cm) furnishing fabric
A cushion pad 1-2in (2.5-5cm) larger than the finished cushion

1 Follow the instructions for inset cushions with mitred corners to make the cushion front, taking care to match stripes or checks if that is what you are using.

2 Cut a back panel the same size as the front, place them right sides together, stitch the bottom and two sides but leave the top open. Turn right sides out.

3 Because the top of these cushions are tied together you need to make a flap inside to tuck the cushion pad into, rather like a pillowcase has, so that the cushion pad does not show. Cut a piece of fabric about 4in (10 cm) deep and the same width as your cushion to make this flap. Make four ties and pin them two to the back and two to the front.

4 Pin the flap to the back over the two ties and cut a second narrower strip to face the front with and pin on in the same way. Stitch these seams.

5 Turn the flap in and secure to the side seam once you have finished off the bottom edge. Turn in the facing on the front of your cushion and stitch down. Insert the cushion pad and tie the two bows.

A Simple Quilted Fold-over Front Purse

YOU WILL NEED

Lining
Outer fabric (you may use the same for lining)
Wadding (batting)
Satin bias binding

This basic shape has been used for several projects in this book: the project folder on page 98, the make-up purses and tiny wedding ring purse in the alphabets section and the handkerchief purse on page 50. As all these projects vary in size, I am not including specific instructions; but they do all follow exactly the same method.

1 Decide what size you would like the purse to be and cut a piece of wadding (batting) that is exactly the same width but three times the length to allow for the folding.

2 Cut a piece of lining the same size as your wadding. The outer piece will have your embroidered panel in it so you will need to adjust the size of the panel to accommodate the embroidery.

3 Stitch the embroidery to the outer fabric to make a panel piece the same size as the wadding (batting).

4 Lay the lining wrong side up on the table, followed by the wadding (batting) and then cover with the outer fabric with the embroidery in it. Pin these three layers together and sew around the edge.

5 Fold the piece into three equal sections and mark the folds. Stitch a straight line across where these folds are. These two lines are the folds at the top and bottom of your purse.

6 Bind the inner edge and then sew up the side seams of the purse with wrong sides together (ie the seam is on the outside).

7 Trim the corners of the flap to make gentle curves. Now bind up one side of the purse around the curved flap and down the other side of the purse all in one length of binding.

8 Take care when starting and finishing as you will need to turn in a short length of binding. You may like to add a button and loop or a press stud on the front flap to keep the purse closed.

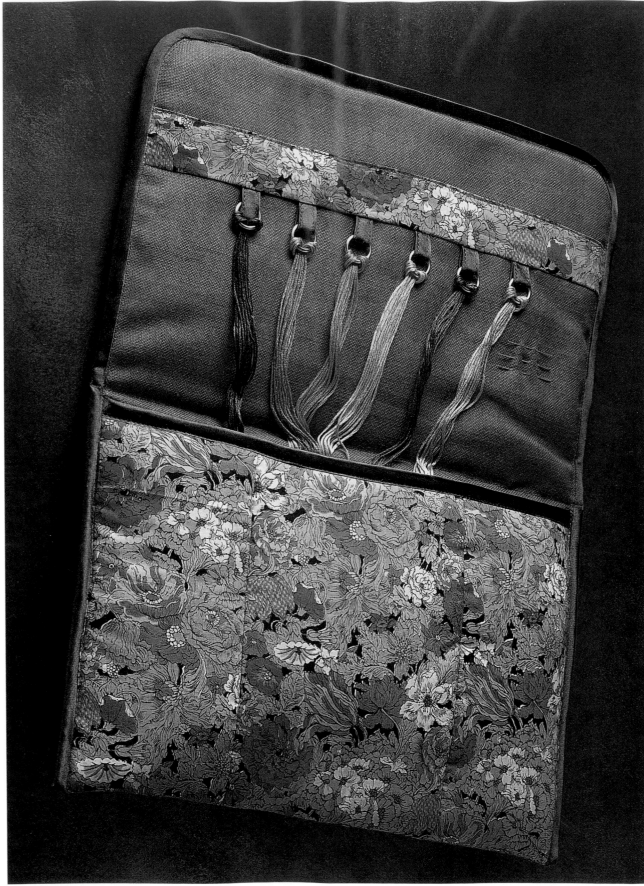

Making Cords and Tassels

Furnishing shops stock a wide variety of trimmings, but you can save a lot of money and gain satisfaction from making your own. You will also get a perfect colour match if you use the same threads that you used for the embroidery.

TWISTED OR MONK'S CORD

This is a simple but effective cord. It can be made with wool (yarn) or stranded cotton (floss), and can be thick and multi-coloured or thin and plain.

1 Decide how long and how thick you want the cord to be. You will require enough strands to make half the desired thickness. They should be three times the desired length.

2 Tie a knot at both ends. Secure one end to a door knob or hook (or persuade a friend to hold it). Twist the other end until the yarn begins to double back on itself when you let the tension off slightly.

3 Fold in half, letting go of the centre point carefully and holding the two ends together. The cord will twist, and you should tie the loose ends together without letting them go.

4 If you need to cut the cord, make sure the end is knotted or the cord will unravel.

5 If you require a thicker cord, start with a longer length and twist and fold twice. If you want to use twists of different colours you have to make two half thickness cords and then join them together so that the twist runs in the same direction all along the length, and then twist again and fold.

When making cords for cushions you will find that the lengths get very long before you twist and fold. I often end up going out the door and into the garden to make the first twists!

Experiment for yourself with these cords. They are great fun to make and can save you a lot of money, not to mention save the time you would have spent searching the shops for a good colour match.

TASSELS

1 Cut a piece of card a little longer than the required length of the tassel.

2 Wind the thread around this until the bundle is the right thickness.

3 Tie together firmly at one end of the card and cut all the threads at the other.

4 Take another length of thread and wind it around all the threads to make the knob at the top of the tassel. Finish off securely.

5 Trim the ends of the tassel to the required length, neatening the end.

6 Use the tie at the top to fasten to the corner of the cushion or around the cord on a cushion. As with cords, the tassels can be thick or thin and plain or multi-coloured.

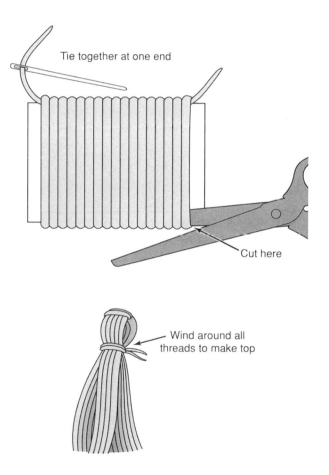

Tie together at one end

Cut here

Wind around all threads to make top

Opposite: Xeranthemum project folder (see page 98).

Suppliers

STRANDED COTTON (FLOSS),
FABRIC AND CANVAS
DMC Creative World Ltd,
Pullman Road, Wigston,
Leicestershire LE18 2DY
Tel: 01533 811040
DMC Corporation, Port
Kearny, Building 10, South
Kearny, New Jersey, USA
Tel: 201-589-0606
DMC Needlecraft Pty Ltd, PO
317 Earlswood, NSW, Australia
Tel: 612 5593 088

APPLETON YARN
Appleton Bros, Thames Works,
Church Street, Chiswick,
London W4 2PE
Potpourri Etc, PO Box 78,
Redondo Beach, Ca. 90277,
USA
Clifton H Joseph & Son
(Australia) Pty. Ltd, 391–393
Little Lonsdale St, Melbourne,
Victoria 3000

LINENS AND EVENWEAVES
Fabric Flair Ltd, Northlands
Industrial Estate, Copheap
Lane, Warminster, Wiltshire
BA12 0BG
Tel: 01985 846400
Zweigart & Sawitzki, Postfach
120, 71043 Sindelfingen,
Germany

LIBERTY FABRICS
Liberty plc, 210–220 Regent
Street, LondonW1R 6AH
Tel: 0171 734 1234
Liberty of London Inc, 108
West 39th St, New York, NY
10018 USA Tel: 212-459-0080
Norman Vivian Pty Ltd, 18
Belmore Street, Surry Hills,
NSW 2010, Australia
Tel: 2 212 1633

VICTORIAN ETUI KIT
Pauline's Patchwork, Swiss
Cottage, Milton Abbas,
Blandford, Dorset DT11 0BJ
Tel: 01258 880852

SLIPPER KIT
Fancy Footwork, PO Box 3207,
London E9 7UA

INLAID FOOTSTOOL
Macgregor Designs, PO Box
129, Burton-upon-Trent
DE14 3XH

HAND MIRROR AND
CHRISTMAS TREASURE BOX
Roland Bartlett, 25 Poplar
Avenue, Markfield LE67 9WP

GOLD NEEDLES
AND STITCHING PAPER
The Inglestone Collection,
Yells Yard, Cirencester Road,
Fairford, Gloucestershire
GL7 4BS
Tel: 01285 712778

ROUND FRAMES AND
WOODEN PINCUSHION BASES
Turnstyle, Alstons, Preston
Wynne, Hereford HR1 3PA
Tel: 01432 820505

Sue Hawkins and Needleworks

Sue's interest in embroidery and
treasured textiles began while
she was working with an
antique dealer who specialized
in 17th-century embroidery. It is
from these early pieces that her
own designs later evolved. In
1991 she sold her needlework
shop in Cheltenham to concen-
trate on designing for her own
company, Needleworks, and
teaching small workshops at
home. She became Technical

Director of the Cross Stitch
Guild founded in 1996 by Jane
Greenoff, and teaches workshops at national shows and
needlecraft shops throughout
the country for the Cross Stitch
Guild and on her own behalf.

Needleworks produces counted
canvaswork, crewelwork and
cross stitch kits. Ask your local
shop for details or write (enclosing a stamped addressed enve-
lope) to:

Needleworks, The Old
Schoolhouse, Hall Road,
Leckhampton, Cheltenham,
Gloucestershire GL53 0HP
Telephone: 0242 584424.

THE CROSS STITCH GUILD

Jane Greenoff founded the Guild in
1996 to promote the enjoyment of
counted needlework of all kinds.
Guild membership has the benefits of
regular journals, study folios, access to
the Guild Members Room at
Longleat and discounts from the
Guild's retail partners. Members can
contribute to influence various parts
of the needlework industry – design,
manufacture, retailing and publishing
etc, but also share the fun of it all
with other stitchers, hence the Guild
motto 'Together, We Count'.
For details of subscriptions, members facilities and any other details
contact:
The Cross Stitch Guild,
The Stable Courtyard,
Longleat House,
Warminster BA12 7NW

Acknowledgements

Once again my thanks must go to my husband, John, and to my daughters, Hannah and Jo for their support and infinite patience with me – it can't always have been easy!

Also to Jane and Bill Greenoff: Jane for a friendship that enriches my life and Bill for … well … being Bill!

To the stitchers without whom I could never have done it all. They are Kathy Elliott, Trina Tait, Olive McAnerney, Jenny Baker and Caroline Gibbons.

To all the ladies who come to weekly classes at my house. They are too many to list but they know who they are. I constantly try out new designs on them and they are always generous with their own ideas and suggestions. My weeks would not be the same without them.

To Cheryl Brown at David & Charles for her enthusiasm for this book and for not panicking when it was a little late!

To Tim and Zöe Hill for their stunning photography.

To Ethan Danielson for transforming the charts and Kay Ball for putting it all together.

To Appletons for their wonderful colours and Zweigart for generous supplies of linen.

To The Inglestone Collection for the beautiful Sewing Coffer pictured on page 21 and the thread winders that go with it.

To Fabric Flair for unlimited Jobelan fabric and the Kit Company for taking over the manufacture of most of my kits at a critical time.

Finally, to Woody, my spaniel, and Stumpy and Ambrose, my cats, who kept me company for hours while I worked and only disturbed me a little with their snoring and dreaming!

The silk cord and pelmet pictured on page 11 and on back of jacket respectively were kindly supplied by the Gallery of Antique Costume & Textiles, 2 Church Street, Marylebone, London NW8 8ED (Tel: 0171 723 9981).

Index

Page references in *italics* indicate illustrations.